BREAKING THE CHAINS

CIRCLES

TAMMY FLOWERS-HOLLIS

Tammy Flowers-Hollis

I have tried to recreate events, locales, and conversations from my memories of them. In order to maintain their anonymity in some instances, I have changed the names of individuals and places. I may have changed some identifying characteristics and details such as physical properties, occupations, and places of residence.

For permission requests, write to the publisher, addressed:
Jacinth Media Productions
52 N. 2nd Street
Coplay, PA 18037

All Scripture quotes are taken from the Holy Bible, King James Version, Cambridge, 1769; and The ESV® Bible
(The Holy Bible, English Standard Version®).
ESV® Text Edition: 2016. Copyright © 2001 by Crossway,
A publishing ministry of Good News Publishers.

Library of Congress Control Number: 2023912416
Paperback ISBN-13: 978-1-9605940-8-2
Hardback ISBN-13: 978-1-960594-09-9
Digital Online ISBN: 978-1-960594-10-5
This book was printed in the United States
First Printing
10 9 8 7 6 5 4 3 2 1
Book cover design by Jacinth Media Productions

You can follow Tammy through her website and social media handles. She is a big advocate for domestic violence, and if you ever feel that your life is in danger *Don't Wait!* Call the **National Domestic Violence Hotline at: (800) 799-7233**

Table of Content

Dedication

I dedicate this book to all women who have suffered and may suffer from domestic violence and other abuse. Just know you are not alone. For I am you, and you are me. I represent you, "the voice of the voiceless." I represent those of you who have been silenced by their abuse, trauma, hurt, torment, and betrayals. We have been told we were uneducated, failures, and not good enough. But no more will your suffering go unnoticed.

I stand as an extraordinary woman with an extraordinary heart building other extraordinary women to share their hearts to keep building and never to teardown. Never accept less than how God has created us. For we are fearfully and wonderfully made.

To the strongest and bravest woman, I know, my mother! It's because of your strength, love for God, and your determination that I am the woman that you see today. Thank you for showing me what a survivor looks like. You are so amazing, and I am so proud to be called your daughter. I love you for life.

Excerpts from my new Single "*I WIN*" 2023:

Hold your head up!
Stick your chest out!
You've got this.
God will see you through!
Walk in your victory!
Talk in your victory!
Move in your victory!
You Win!

Introduction

Today, I stand boldly against generational curses, domestic violence, and the many hidden secrets that have plagued my family and loved ones for too long. I, Tammy, invite you to take this journey with me. Gather your tissues, popcorn, and pom-poms, as I take you behind the scenes of my life.

The cycle ends here!! As I decree and declare life, healing, prosperity, peace, love, and victory over my life. Together, let us go beyond the limitations of the past and embrace a future defined by resilience and triumph.

I am taking my power back and invite you to do the same!

CIRCLES

Chapter 1

What A Life

While I was constantly exposed to violence from a young age, it wasn't until I was four that I started to understand it. On October 3, 1976, my parents Debra Simpson and Darryl King welcomed me into the world in Camden, South Carolina. My parents met in high school through a mutual buddy, and my mother had already had a child when they met. My dad was known for riding his bike around Kirkwood in Camden, South Carolina while carrying a shotgun. According to my mom, she and my dad never really went on a real date, just to church.

Eventually, my mother became pregnant with me. Because she was still quite young, now with two children, she went to stay with her mother so that she would have additional help. The help only a mother could give. My mother stayed with my grandmother for one month. Soon as one month passed, my father ordered my mother back home.

My father then advised my mother to marry him. She wasn't in love with my father and did not have the desire to spend the rest of her life with him. But, because my mother was not as educated in the legal field, my father told her that he could take me away from her if she did not marry him. Reluctantly, she said yes, and they were married on February 24, 1977. My mother did not know that she had more authority than he led on. My grandmother paid for my mother to give birth to me. This meant my grandmother paid for the ownership of me.

After my mother returned home with my older brother and me, my father left, went north for several months, and did not return until December 25, 1977. Without my father's presence, my grandmother would pay rent, which was forty-nine dollars. Even though the house had already been furnished, my mother worked so she could add more to the house.

After a while, she bought a three-piece gold living room set comprising a sofa, a loveseat, and a chair.

When my father returned and saw that life was moving on without him, he became jealous and angry. He took the table from the dining room and blocked the kitchen so that my mother could not run out the front door. However, she did run out the back screen door wearing only her gown, running barefoot until she reached the baseball field. My father caught up with her on the baseball field and picked her up to carry her back home. When they reached the house, my father placed something in front of the door. He then went into the bedroom, picked my mother up, and slammed her body onto the cold wooden floor. Then he snatched her up and hit her so hard in her face that her face hit the corner of the bedroom door, cutting the corner of her right eye. The cut was bleeding so much that she had to be taken to the hospital.

My mother walked into the hospital with a towel pressed against her face, making the best attempt to cover the deep cut. Still, the blood continued to pour out and refused to be hidden. She could soon see with her one good eye a woman, accompanied by her husband, who had been long-time friends with her mother. Embarrassed and quiet, my mother walked past them with her eye swollen and blackened, hoping they would not say anything to bring attention to my father.

Later, my grandmother confronted my mother about her having to go to the hospital. They realized it was too dangerous for her to stay, so my mother returned to live with my grandmother. Despite all the circumstances, my mother held on to her faith and continued attending church.

Eventually, my mother returned home because she did not want to bring problems to my grandmother's home. My mother tried her best to deal with the many violent issues. There would be some good days, but bad days would become worse. During it all, my mother found herself with child once again.

CIRCLES

My father stopped going to church and attempted to stop her. She would come home from church, and my father would have all his drinking buddies there. A woman once would drink with him at the house, and one day, she asked to hold my little brother. My mother, of course, said, "No," and my father again became angry.

My mother had worked for a while, and with my grandmother's help, she furnished the house to make it more of a home. One day, my father decided to sell two of our beds and keep one mattress. My grandmother had purchased those beds. Before we knew it, we were moving once again.

My mother worked, and my father drank and roamed the streets. Soon, there was insufficient money to keep a roof over our heads and food on the table. My grandmother spoke to a man that had a house available. Even though the house was not in good shape, he allowed us to live there because it was a storage house.

We could see between the boards on the floor of the house to the partial concrete and dirt that lie under it. We were so poor we could not afford lights or a stove. My mother cooked food on a fireplace, and we all slept in one full-sized bed.

One night my older brother had an accident and peed in the bed, so my father sent him to a separate room where he would now sleep on the bare floor, cold and lonely. I could see the hurt in my mother's eyes, not knowing if her son was freezing to death in the other room or if snakes would bite him.

The winter was moving in quickly, and a serious struggle remained. We now had no food, wood, or coal. My father broke up the last bed frame and used it as firewood to keep us warm. My mother was now at her breaking point, and she took my father to court to have him removed from the home. The courts granted my mother's request.

My father had become angry because pride took over, even though people knew of his violence. It was as if my mother had let the cat out of the bag. It was embarrassing for him, and he became angry enough to kill. He sat down on the porch of his brother's home and began to load a shotgun while he expressed outwardly in front of his niece Tramaine that he would kill my mother. This was the day that he would blow her away, never to return.

Chapter 2

Goodbye Camden

Tramaine tried not to show emotions in front of my father so that he would not be aware of her soon-to-be rescue. She walked out of the yard and down the hill towards my grandmother's home, where she knew she would find my mother. She had advised my mother that my father was loading his shotgun and aiming to kill her. My grandmother, Bessie, heard the disturbing news and realized that my Aunt Mattie, who lived in New York, had sent her money to pay for her life insurance policy.

My grandmother understood that this man did not just talk; he was about action. So, she had to move quickly and could not take the risk of processing her movements for too long. She took my little brother's milk bottle sitting on the counter in the kitchen and poured fresh milk into the bottle, not removing the old, spoiled milk already within the bottle. She then went to the back room, grabbed a coat left behind by my cousin Petra, and placed it on my oldest brother, Robert. My little brother Jonathan and I had to share a blanket. My grandmother also found some stale donuts and placed them inside a brown paper bag for us to eat.

Bessie understood that time was of the essence, but believed God would make everything work out. To see and remember her faith, to move with such ease in times of trouble, would always be remembered. Bessie was smart and knew that my father would see us once she loaded us into my Aunt Darla's car. She placed my mother, my two brothers, and me on the back seat floor and advised us to lie low and still. She then placed my four-year-old cousin in the seat behind the passenger. Bessie then sat in the front seat, and Darla would be the driver. As we began driving past my Uncle Tony's home, my father stood up only to see my Aunt Darla driving, my grandmother in the front passenger seat, and my cousin Kaitlyn in the back seat. He then sat back down and continued to get his shotgun ready for war.

My Aunt Darla drove us all the way from Camden, South Carolina, to Sumter, South Carolina, on the floor of her car. My mother knew that if my father did not see my aunt's car, he would soon start looking. We went to a family friend's home, and she gave my Aunt Darla her car keys so we could continue the travel by switching vehicles. My Aunt Darla then drove us all the way to Columbia, South Carolina, to the Greyhound Bus Station, where my grandmother used my Aunt Mattie's insurance money to buy three one-way tickets to New York. The plan was that we would now live with my aunt in New York, never to return to Camden, South Carolina.

My grandmother placed us on the bus, and I can only imagine the many thoughts and emotions that were going through her mind, but she would only allow us to see her strength. My mother located seats towards the back of the bus. Even though my grandmother paid for three seats, my mother would not allow us to have any space from her, so the four of us stayed within two seats. I can hear my mother's heartbeat racing faster and faster as her body shakes from fear. Fear of knowing he can locate us on that bus and still kill her. We were not out of the woods yet.

Finally, the bus driver got aboard the bus, and the look in my mother's eyes would never be forgotten. Where she was born and raised, the only place she ever knew, her home, to never see it again. What if she never saw her mother again? What if he goes after her mother to try to get to her? So much, Lord, how much can one person take? The driver sat in his seat, and a noise came out, sounding like steam.

12

CIRCLES

The bus then jerked, and our little bodies went forward, then back. My mother instructed us to get down on the floor. We could not risk my father seeing us or even someone that may know him. As we all lay low towards the floor, people would look, not understanding our trauma and not knowing that this was a drastic change for all of us. This was a change in our history.

The bus slowly pulled out, and my mother held us tighter. There were so many emotions. Fear, anger, confusion, doubt, defeat, and victory, but she just held on. She kept us low until we reached a city where no one would recognize us. Then she allowed us to slowly climb back into the seat but remained close to her bosom.

Even though she allowed us to look out the window now and again, she would not get off the bus at rest stops because she knew to still be careful. We just could not take any risk. As time would pass now, we were hungry. My mother reached over and pulled out the brown paper bag that my grandmother had given her, pulled out a couple of stale donuts, and gave them to my brother, Robert, and me. We knew not to complain because we did not want my mother to become hurt more than she already was. So, we slowly took bites and hoped it would stay down and remove the hunger. After a couple of bites, I looked up at my mother and smiled, hoping to make her believe everything was okay. But I knew that even when she smiled back at me, her smile had such emptiness.

She turned her head towards the window, and the tears began to flow down her cheek. Maybe she thought of herself as a failure. Maybe she realized that she would now be by herself with three children. How would we survive? I didn't know, but I was sure I was glad to have my mother. As the tears flowed, my brothers and I held on to our mother and went to sleep hoping that when we would awake, this would all be over.

Chapter 3

Welcome To New York

Finally, we arrived at 42nd Street, also known as Times Square, at the bus terminal called The Port Authority. Everywhere you looked, every space was filled with people of all colors, shapes, and sizes. People were lying on the ground; some looked dirty and clean. There were smells I had never smelled before, and I couldn't tell if it was a pleasant or bad smell, but I knew we were no longer in Camden, South Carolina.

I then saw an unfamiliar face, but my mother seemed familiar with it. It was my Aunt Mattie, my mother's sister, we would live with. My aunt walked towards me with a smile and gently stuck her hand out. I did not remember meeting her before, but I felt it was okay to grab onto her. I slowly slid my hand into the middle of her palm and held her hand. We all walked out into the bright, crowded streets of New York. I was so amazed by all the lights and performances people put on in the streets. They did not wait to go into a theatre and perform on stage, but the streets of New York were their stage. They sang, danced, painted pictures of other people, and expressed no tiredness. Yep, I was amazed, cold, and hungry.

My Aunt held my hand as she walked to the corner and stuck out her other hand. A yellow car pulled up in front of us. My Aunt advised my mother to get into the car's back seat with my brothers and me as she proceeded to get in the front with the driver. She then instructed the driver to take us to Edgecombe Avenue in Harlem, New York. I could tell he was a pro at getting people where they needed to go on time because the car began going extremely fast, dipping, and dodging through other cars as if we were the untouchables.

We arrived at the infamous Edgecombe Avenue in Harlem, New York. This building had six floors, three apartments on each floor, and we

CIRCLES

were now going to live on the third floor in apartment 8. I had never seen a building so tall, as I was only familiar with houses.

Chapter 4

Why Did You Let Him In?

I always wanted to sing and found myself always humming a tune. I would play church with my brothers; I was the singer, and my brothers would preach or play the drums on the shoe box. Sometimes we would switch, and I would be the preacher but remained the singer. So, continuing at four years old, I began going to Paradise Baptist Church with my aunt Mattie. My aunt was an awesome choir director. She expressed such seriousness in her teaching but was easy to talk to. She directed the youth choir as well as the senior and mid-aged choir. I did not understand everything about church and sometimes struggled to stay awake while the preacher preached, but I knew music.

They placed me in the youth choir that my aunt taught because I could retain the notes given. I could also hear the harmony by this time and would not get confused with other sections singing. Soon, I found myself standing on a table or on the upper stairs near the pulpit, either leading the choir or singing a solo. I remember the church taking up an offering for me after I had sung and presented the money to my aunt. After the service, my brother and I would have the best lunch. My oldest brother and I attended that church for approximately two years.

My mother started calling down south to check on my grandmother. She wanted to know if my father had sought revenge. He did! My father had gone to my grandmother's home and threatened all the many things he would do if she did not tell him where we were. I can imagine the fear that ran through my grandmother, but she never told him.

One day, he went into my grandmother's backyard where the outhouse was and poured gasoline all around it. He then lit it on fire, burning it to the ground along with our only toilet. My grandmother was visibly angry but still trusted God and would not bow down to the enemy and his threats. The devil has limitations! This took strength, courage, and faith in God to understand the power that God has provided and that lies within.

More time passed and seemingly the craziness had managed to calm down. My mother became curious about my father's whereabouts again and whether his behavior had changed. My mother reached out to his mother and left a phone number where she could be reached. Shortly, my father called back, and he and my mother now attempted to reconcile their marriage. She believed he had changed, so she gave him our new address because my aunt had moved out. So, my father came from South Carolina and moved in with us.

All seemed to be going well briefly until my father showed that he never stopped drinking. My mother found empty liquor bottles under the tub, behind the toilet, under the beds, and even behind the radiator. In the past, my mother would call the police to escort him out of the apartment and they would just tell him to take a walk and cool down. That never helped. It just prolonged her punishment for when he would return. He stood over her with a pot of scolding hot water and threatened to pour it on her while she lay in bed.

But this time, my mother gained enough strength to say no more and kicked my father out. He left for a few days, but then she started receiving phone calls advising that he had seen the light and desired to change. It was quite easy for him to incorporate God's name into the conversation to make my mother feel like she was the bad guy, and that God was not pleased with her actions. Even though she tried to stand her ground, eventually she gave in. My father stated that he just wanted to see his children and then he would leave.

My mother opened the door and allowed my father to come in. She told him we were in the bedroom watching the television. My father came into the bedroom and spoke to me and my two brothers but then proceeded to walk out of the bedroom. He made a detour towards the kitchen where my mother was cooking. He then reached and pulled a knife out of the dish rack and as my mother continued to tend to her meal, she felt warmness run down her back.

The things that surrounded her in the kitchen began to fade away. She did not know that the knife my father held just pierced her in her back and through her right lung. My mother slid down to the floor as the blood traced the tiles in the kitchen. She dared not scream because she needed to make my father believe that she would not survive this cowardly act. She slowly dragged her almost lifeless body to the opening between the kitchen and the foyer, trying to confirm that my father had left.

Once she could see that he was gone, she called out for my oldest brother. I then heard him scream and cry out at the top of his lungs. Meanwhile, my mother remained calm and instructed my brother to go and knock on the super's door. Mr. Bobby lived next door to us. She continued to press her way towards the front door and now I found myself at the age of six, watching the dark burgundy blood flow out of my mother. The blood oozing from her body left a bloody trail on the tiles of the building hallway.

Mr. Bobby answered his door and immediately saw my mother lying in the corner of the hallway, struggling to breathe. He then ran back into his apartment and grabbed the phone to call the ambulance.

Mr. Bobby's wife stood holding their apartment door open, watching, crying, and screaming. She then said I knew something like this would eventually happen. Did I mention that my mother was pregnant with my little brother at the time of the stabbing?

Well, she was. The ambulance came, and they placed an oxygen mask over my mother's face as another paramedic attempted to stop her from bleeding out.

CIRCLES

They placed my mother on the stretcher, but the puddles of blood remained, together with all the many tools and gadgets used to save her life. I just sat there and watched, unable to move a limb. I felt helpless, lost, scared, but most of all, confused. Why Mama did you trust anything that man said? Could you not feel the evil that ran through his pores?

My father was now on the run but decided not to run with the knife. He threw the knife in the sewage drain in front of the building in hopes that it would wash far away but the police were able to retrieve it, but not him.

Meanwhile, my brothers and I were taken to my Uncle Ray and Aunt Dorothy's home while the adults tried to figure out whether my mother would live. Finally, a face I recognized all my life. It was my grandma, Bessie. She found out what happened to my mother and rushed to be by her side and to ensure we were taken care of.

I desired so much to focus strictly on my mother's recovery, but that became quite impossible. I was being molested since the age of five. So, instead of a 6-year-old girl worrying if her mommy will return to her, she now remains on the line of defense. My body was not penetrated but violated. I could not understand why such a gruesome act had to take place. What about me turned you on? Please tell me so that I can turn it off. Was it normal to be with a male and a female?

Ok, ok so now time to put back on the front because today we have to go to the hospital to see my mother. The door to my mother's hospital room was pushed open and I began to slowly walk in. I saw a hard clear plastic, rectangular-shaped box on the floor with a plastic circular tube coming out of it and it was routed through my mother's left side. Inside the box was my mother's blood, and it was moving up towards the inside of my mother, and then I would see it return to the box. It looked like my mother's blood was being purified. She did not want me to worry, so she pulled the sheets up higher so that I would not see into her side. So, I played along and remained blind.

My mother then said, "Guess what? You now have another little brother!" That made me incredibly happy and now I could put aside all the things that were hurting me at that moment. Eventually, my mother came home from the hospital with my baby brother, and he looked like an absolute doll baby. His hair was so full and curly, and he would always laugh.

Somehow, I still managed to go to school through all that life was dealing me. I was attending Mahalia Jackson Elementary School, also known as P.S.123. Once I began the second grade, my father attempted to enter our lives again. He called my mother and advised her that he would no longer bother her if he could have his children. Of course, my mother feared for her life, and she felt that he would not hurt his children, so she made an exchange. We had now moved from apartment number eight to seven.

My father came knocking on the door and my mother had pulled her brown wooden coffee table that normally sat in the center of her living room against the door. She slid my brothers and me out the door one by one, careful not to open the door too much. I was 7 years old; my brother Jonathan was 4, and Shane was just turning 2. My father had no car, so the New York trains took him everywhere. He placed my legs around his neck, allowing them to dangle towards his chest, past his shoulders. He then carried my brothers in his arms. We rode the train for approximately two hours into the midnight hour until we reached Brooklyn, New York.

My father then made us walk with him to the projects, where we met a lady named Sherry. Sherry had a son named Barry, and they introduced him as our brother. I stood puzzled, like how could this be. My birthday was in October and his was the following February. I finally understood that my father was not faithful to my mother. At the time, there were more important things to concentrate on, like food, clean clothes, toilet tissue, and pampers for Shane. I was placed in a bed with my new brother, Barry, as my brothers would be with my father and Barry's mother in another room. I could not sleep knowing what was happening in my life.

CIRCLES

The next morning, Barry's mother sent him to school, and we stayed back with his mother. My father had left us with this lady, this stranger. The bathroom tissue had run out and there was not enough food and pampers. I became creative and wrapped Shane in the newspaper to prevent him from using the bathroom on the floor. The lady asked me, "Do you know your mother's phone number?" I quickly answered yes and began to call out my phone number. This sweet lady dialed the numbers, and I heard my mother's voice. Barry's mother advised my mother that we were safely in Brooklyn with her. She proceeded to tell my mother that my father was not present at the time.

My mother asked to speak with me. Sherry passed me the phone as she became the lookout. My mother said hello and I could hear such pain and distress in her voice, and I just knew that I had to somehow make her feel better. I did not become emotional but stern in my speaking. I advised her that we were doing great, that Sherry was doing a great job with us, and that she was not to worry because we would be home soon. I did not know at that time if that was true, but I did not want to believe otherwise.

The day has now passed, and the night has fallen. My father still did not return, so Sherry cared for us to the best of her ability, just like she had told my mother she would. It was now time for bed and even though I did not want to close my eyes, I couldn't help it because I watched over my brothers all day. I could no longer keep my eyes open. At about one o'clock in the morning, I felt a cool breeze brush over me as I tried to sleep. It was Sherry, opening the front door for my father. I pretended to remain asleep as they would go back and forth on why he was not there and why she was placed in a position to take care of us.

As they continued to speak, I heard fear in Sherry's voice. She would do what I have learned so well, which is back down and now present a calm tone, hoping not to upset my father. She allowed him to think that he was right and that there was no reason to feel threatened. My father was like an animal, whereas if in his mind his back was up against the wall that gave him good reason to attack physically.

Chapter 5

There's No Place Like Home

The next morning, my father woke me up and instructed me to get dressed and to dress my brothers. We were taken outside and back on the train towards Harlem, New York without eating. We got off at the stop up the hill from my home, 145th Street. This hill was known as the "Jamaican Hill" simply because the Jamaicans controlled that part of the block. My father proceeded down the hill with me and my brothers toward what I called my home. Soon a man approached us, and I did not understand what was happening. Still, I was awfully familiar with the spirit my father was showing.

Whatever was said at that time was enough to bring out the anger in my father. He had such a calmness in him, but deadly. He then told me to watch my brothers. I understood that my father's choice of weapon was knives, so without hesitation, he placed the man in a headlock using his right arm and with his left hand, the knife went from right to left. He dragged him behind the two bushes on the right-hand side of this building. He stood tall and remained calm, walking towards me and my brothers. We continued to walk down the hill after he looked at me and said, "Daddy loves you."

We sat outside my building for a huge part of the day, but my mother was nowhere in sight. Eventually, we walked back to the train station, taking another route. My father took us to the train station and stood by a pay phone. He then advised me that he was going to get something and that he would be right back. So, I took my brother's hands and held them close to me. We would see people walking in and out of the train station, but my father still did not return.

Two police officers approached my brothers and me and asked who we were with. I guess someone called them because we were there by ourselves for over an hour. They asked me where my mother was, and I answered, "I don't know but my father left us standing here." I told the officer that I knew my telephone number and she took the number from me. Once again, I heard my mother's voice as she spoke with the police officer. She first requested that my mother identify all three of her children and was finally able to tell my mother where we were and that they would bring us to her.

When the police officers arrived at my mother's home, she answered the door with tears in her eyes. She just kept saying thank you to the officers and even more to God. My mother ran bath water because she could tell that we were filthy. She took off all our clothes and threw them in the garbage. Then she gently placed us in the warm water. At this time, it did not matter what our sex was; we had to get cleaned up. Once my mother removed us from the bathtub, a thick black and gray ring surrounded the tub. But we were all simply happy to be with our mother once again.

Chapter 6

Here We Go Again

Somehow, my father landed back in our lives but never stayed because he would constantly be in and out of jail. Yes, you heard me correctly. My father never served time for the stabbing of my mother. He may be the only human who has harmed a person; the law confirms, and he is still set free. I continued going to elementary school where I would sing songs in the Glee Club and became a dancing elf. I was able to teach myself how to tap dance and once they accepted that I was a singer at heart, I would lead songs, too.

With all the ups and downs in my life, it was nearly impossible to continue with Paradise Baptist Church, so my mother started taking me and my brothers to a church much closer to home and much smaller. Shortly after, we became faithful members of St. Michael's Holy Temple. There, I learned more about what God has given me. My mother and I joined "The Voices of New York." This group consists of nothing but females with the ability to sing from Soprano to Bass. I was the youngest in the group, but that did not matter because I was obligated to still pull my own weight. We ministered all over New York, Long Island, The Hamptons, and wherever else they invited us.

The group's founder was named Diana Brown aka Dee Brown, and she was a perfectionist. She trained us to sing acapella in every key. We would sing with perfect harmony, and we understood the importance of listening and matching. I cried at many rehearsals, but my godmother, Dee Brown, was not fazed. She would not allow me to give up or have a pity party. If anything, she worked me harder. My god sister, Nyema was attending a junior high school named Harbor Performing Arts soon to graduate.

This school was designed to increase your performing arts skills.

So, as I was saying, it was soon time to register for junior high school and my godmother advised my mother that it would be best for me to attend Harbor as well. My elementary school did not agree with that because that meant that I would be leaving their district, which also means taking funding away from them. My mother asked me what I wanted to do and of course, I said Harbor.

An audition was scheduled for me for vocals and drama, and I was accepted for both, but vocal would be my major. I was so excited to be able to explore more of my gifts, and now I would be able to sing even more.

My mother was now doing well. She worked while we all attended school. Yes, life was good.

My mother was into Tupperware, so she started selling it on the side. One day, she decided to have a Tupperware party and a lot of women attended. She even had some women that she knew and grew up with from Camden, SC there.

I was 11 years old at the time and while the party was going on, there was a knock on the door. It was my father, his sister, and her children. My father asked my mother if his sister's children could come in and use the bathroom. My mother was very hesitant but also did not want to alarm her guest so she said, "Your sister and her children can come in and use the bathroom, but you have to stay out." The unfortunate reality was his sister knew that he was up to no good and made the attempt to warn my mother while apologizing for coming there. As my aunt and cousins were leaving, my father tried to grab my mother to push her back into the bathroom by herself so that he may be alone with her. Thank God for my aunt being that blockage so he could not accomplish what was on his mind.

Once they left, we were able to get back to selling Tupperware. But because my mother had a visit from my father, she could not be at ease. She felt that he was still lurking around, not far away. Overall, my mother's Tupperware party was an absolute hit. People started to leave because it was getting late.

My mother told me to open the front door to let some of our guests out. I unlocked the door, reached for the doorknob, and suddenly, I felt a quick spark of heat. Flames went up from under the door and then broke through each side of the door melting the locks, paint, and anything that stood in the way.

Everyone started screaming, hoping not to die that night. Some tried to figure out whether we should place energy into stopping the fire, while others accepted defeat and were willing to let everything go so that they would survive.

My mother grabbed the first liquid she could get her hand on, which turned out to be a pitcher of Kool-Aid. She continued to attempt to put the fire out as the other women headed out the window and down the fire escape on the front part of the building. The firefighters arrived, placed a ladder towards the fire escape, and escorted people down. One lady screamed so loud you would have thought she was the only one needing to be rescued.

Finally, we were all able to make it out of the apartment safely. However, all that we have ever owned had now evaporated with this fire. Everything that my mother worked so hard to provide for us, and at times neglected herself just to see a smile on our faces, was gone.

CIRCLES

Once we made it safely to the ground, people stood enraged at my mother. We realized that it was my father that poured gasoline in front of every apartment door totaling eighteen apartments and set each apartment on fire. Everyone survived, but the fire destroyed the apartments' insides and the building's outside structure.

My father was eventually caught and sentenced to 10 years for arson. However, now we had to find somewhere to live. My mother's cousin offered to let us move in with her and because she did not live far from us, we did not have to change our schools.

We started from scratch with our clothes. That's when my mother learned about the many things that could be purchased from a thrift shop for cheap. Even though my father set fire to the building, the landlord stayed faithful to my mother. He and his wife understood that we were victims of domestic violence. He advised my mother that we could move back into the building, back into apartment seven, and even though living with my cousin had been a blessing, I missed home.

We moved back into our old apartment and were constantly reminded of the fire that consumed everything my mother worked for. No more carpets were on the floor, but now we had tiles. The walls were painted white, but the deformity from the fire was still there. The metal that once allowed the door to close was no longer in existence. However, one significant change was now we had a toilet that would flush like regular toilets with a handle. The other toilet was connected to a string from a box on the wall. Sometimes it would work. Most times it would not, so we habitually used a bucket of water to flush the toilet. Even though my life would be considered hell to an outsider, I knew it as just regular ole life.

I did not know this was not how life should be. What others may call surviving; I saw it as I have survived. It was not an option to project the possibility of failure, but we controlled our destiny even if we did not physically see it at that time. It existed because we knew no other way.

Chapter 7

The Show Must Go On

Despite how my seventh-grade year started while attending Harbor Junior High School for the Performing Arts, I could express myself through drama, dance, and music. I was able to act in school plays like The Wiz, The Chorus Line, and Guys and Dolls. I welcomed every opportunity that would allow me to express myself, including singing songs in various languages, opera, and of course, gospel. I attended Harbor for three years.

In my last year of junior high school, I found out that my best friend, who is also my 1st cousin, was diagnosed with breast cancer. Bear in mind, we are only seven months apart. How could that happen? Why did that happen? Those were a few questions that ran through my mind. All I knew was that I wanted to be there for her.

My grandmother had come up to New York from Camden, SC to support me in graduating from the ninth grade. She and my mother decided it would be good if I could go back down south and spend time with my best friend.

This would not be the first time I returned to Camden, SC. My mother allowed me to go and stay with my aunt Darla and my grandmother almost every summer, and for those summers that I stayed in New York, my best friend would come up and stay with me. It was something rare for us to be apart.

When she would visit me, we would roam the streets of New York, eating in restaurants every day. Kaitlyn's father owned a sneaker store on 125th Street which was not too far from the infamous Apollo Theater. He always pulled out an enormous stack of money and gave a good bit to

CIRCLES

Kaitlyn. She never showed a selfish bone in her body. Boy, those were the good ole days.

I remember my mother would provide us with chores to do each day while she went to work. Kaitlyn usually completed her chores early in the day just to get it over with. I, on the other hand, was hardheaded and a procrastinator.

One day, my mother provided instructions on what chores we were responsible for. I found myself just playing around until I realized now the time was drawing near for my mother to be home. I then took hold of the clothes that I was to iron and told Kaitlyn I needed her help. She then reminded me of all the playing that I was doing and now looked forward to my beating.

I continued to beg for help, and I grabbed the broom to scare Kaitlyn and suddenly there was music that came from the television. It was Tom & Jerry and their Uncle Pecos with a long mustache, a huge hat, and his guitar singing something about Hillbilly Jim's go-riding hood combo. We both looked at each other and started laughing. Kaitlyn saved me from a beating.

As time passed on, my mother was still working and providing for the family. She now started dating and in the midst of her life, she blessed me with a little sister. I thought I was happy with my brother Shane, but nothing could compare to having another girl in the house.

I became a babysitter, chef, housekeeper, and a second mother, and for a while, I did not mind. My sister was a living doll baby. I dressed her up in the prettiest clothes and placed pretty bobos and barrettes in her hair. I took her everywhere I went.

People who did not know me thought that I was just another statistic. Just another young teenage mother having a baby and I honestly didn't care because I didn't feel that it was for me to prove differently.

Tammy Flowers-Hollis

So, during the last year of Junior High, they offered me the opportunity to audition for Fiorello H. LaGuardia High School for the Performing Arts and I took it. I auditioned and was accepted for both drama and vocals, but of course, I leaned more toward the vocals. LaGuardia was just like the show "Fame" with Debbie Allen.

Once I came back from down south from spending time with my best friend who had Cancer, I had a fresh look on life and how fragile life was.

I understood that there was no age too young to be hit with such a powerful disease and to live each day as if it were your last. You just do not know. Thankfully, as of to date, she is still here in the land of the living, and she is Cancer free.

Chapter 8

Time To Grow Up

O nce I returned to New York from my summer trip, I was so excited. I was now going to be starting high school and have boyfriends, hang out with friends, and have more say, right?

I started attending LaGuardia high school in September 1991. Day one granted me an opportunity to meet all my teachers, and it allowed me to see some familiar faces from my old junior high school. It was a bit scary going to a school where everyone seemed to be so big, and I was only 4 feet 11 inches tall, but I was determined.

Shortly after attending my new school, one of my music teachers requested that each student come to the front of the class and perform a song of their choice. He wanted us to feel a sense of freedom. I was extremely excited about this opportunity because it would allow me to show what I had and afterward see the amazement in everyone's eyes.

First, I advised my music teacher that I was hoarse, but I will try. I then gave all that I had and began to sing "Amazing Grace." When I finished, all eyes were on me. My teacher stood still and gently pulled on his beard. He then stated that if that is what you call hoarse, I cannot wait to hear your full voice.

I was pleased with myself, and I smiled all the way back to my seat. I must admit I was quite pumped up and then my music teacher made one other comment that followed the praise that he had given me.

He said, "But you will not be doing that in here."

I was curious about what he meant by that comment. I learned that gospel was not what he taught, but opera. I had a taste of this in junior high school, but in high school it was mandatory, and I loved it. I was taught other languages besides English and Spanish. I learned German, French, and Italian.

So, high school was going well, and now I had a boyfriend. His name was Austin, and he was a great guy. We were not only dating but good friends. Austin and I would have a lot of fun together and would somehow remain in each other's presence.

I remember one time my mother stated that she had to go grocery shopping and for me to stay home and babysit my little sister. At this time, I was a bit upset because I felt that I was made a mother before my time. Everyone else around my age seemed to be free. I told Austin I couldn't go anywhere and that I had to stay home with my little sister. He then came to my house to keep me company. I was excited about that.

Now, let me just say that where I lived, we had a serious rat infestation. We were used to functioning with roaches and mice, but rats came with diseases, biting, and aggression. The kind that did not run away from you but welcomed you to walk towards them so that they may attack.

The rats were entering the apartment faster than we could kill and get them out. We could not use glue traps because they would still be able to walk the floor until the trap would fall off or they would bite their own tails off for freedom. My mother had such a fear of what the rats would do to us as her children that she made all four of us sleep in the bed with her, as she would stay awake all night as the lookout.

So, fast forward, now I was babysitting my sister and hanging out with my boyfriend. I began to feel sick, and Austin was helpful and nurturing. He would always look out for me first. He stood up and looked at me.

"I'm going to make you some soup," he said, then proceeded to the kitchen and reached to turn on the light from the string that hung from the ceiling, and at the same time he was reaching into the kitchen cabinet. He was finally able to turn on the light and when the light came on with his hand still lying on the cabinet shelf, I was able to see a huge black sewage rat sitting comfortably by his hand. I didn't want to scare him too badly, but I did need to rescue him. At first, I tried to speak to him in a calm voice, but that did not work, so I kindly yelled the words, "Turn around! It's a rat."

Quickly, he turned around, and the rat started to hiss at him. He moved quickly, screaming at the top of his lungs, sounding like a girl, and jumping up and down. Suddenly, I lost my appetite for soup, and he lost the desire to go back into the kitchen. Austin walked over to me, kissed my cheek, and walked straight out the front door. Shortly afterward, Austin and I broke up.

Finally, my mother came home, and I was so excited because my Uncle Seth, who is my mother's brother, was living with us and he was from Camden, so I seriously believed he knew how to cook. Seth said if I was still awake when he got home, he would make some fried green tomatoes. I've never eaten fried green tomatoes before, not to mention I'd never seen green tomatoes.

They brought the grocery bags into the house and my Uncle Seth showed me the green tomatoes. He then took out the cooking oil, flour, salt, pepper, and a frying pan. He placed the oil in the pan and allowed the oil to heat up. He then rinsed the tomatoes and cut them into big rings. He seasoned the tomatoes and dipped each ring into the flour. He pulled each ring up out of the flour and shook off the excess flour and placed it into the frying pan.

My mouth watered just to look at the process and to smell the seasonings all mashed together. I could tell this was going to be the best meal ever. Then my Uncle Seth asked if I was ready to eat. I didn't have to answer because my plate was already in my hands, moving towards him. He took a spatula and carefully laid the golden brown perfectly cut tomato ring on my plate. I walked slowly to the dining table, making sure not to drop the perfection of a meal.

I gently placed my plate on the table, pulled out my fork and knife, and laid it on my napkin that rested on the table. I joined my hands together for prayer and kept one eye open to make sure my food would remain on my plate during the prayer. I said my Amens and slowly pierced the tomato with my fork to hold it in place. I then slowly picked up my butter knife and began to cut closest to the teeth of my fork on each side.

Finally, a nice piece of the juicy, well-seasoned, home-cooked green tomato was ready to be placed in my mouth. As I lift my fork upwards towards my mouth, I can feel my mouth watering, almost drooling. I allowed that tomato to touch my lips with the newly cooked heat. I continued to insert it until I felt the tomato land on my tongue. No longer could I wait. No longer could I bear the suspense. I bit down through that tomato ring not once, not twice, but three times. I then swallowed this "amazing" green tomato as the tears fell from my eyes. My uncle then said, "How is it?"

I let out the biggest voice ever and said, "THIS IS ABSOLUTELY HORRIBLE! I stayed up for this? Goodnight!!!"

My mother continued working as a home attendant. She now had a new patient, and he was a minister in his church, and he was sightless. He would minister to my mother and because she was his home attendant, she would now be responsible for him getting to his church service on Sundays.

One Sunday my mother escorted him to his service at the Garden of Prayer COGIC in the Bronx, New York and when she came home, she was so excited about attending there that the next Sunday she took my two younger brothers and my little sister. I did not attend immediately because I was more interested in what the world had to offer. I found myself mixed in with what's called the "wrong crowd."

However, I could never blame anyone else for the choice I've made because after the constant spiritual teachings from my mother, not to mention the many trials God had delivered me and my family from, I made my own decisions. I began fighting, drinking alcohol, smoking cigarettes, weed, and being promiscuous. I honestly did not know what love really was. I didn't know me. It was more important for a man to say that he loved me than my understanding that I didn't even love me.

My understanding of love was sex. If he was being treated better than he had ever been treated before, why wouldn't he love me, right? Feeding him, pleasing him in the bed, buying him gifts, and pumping up his ego, he should fall head over hill in love with me, right? I was different, right? No other female could do what I was doing, right?

I have been told by my peers that I was different and that I didn't fit in with them, but that only made me work harder to prove that I was just like them. I would party every chance I got but there would always be a voice lingering in my head and I would fight against it. I knew that it was right, but I was too young to settle down, right? That was what older folks did when they already lived their life, right?

So, eventually, at the age of 16, I decided to visit The Garden of Prayer COGIC. It was quite good, I thought. There were so many young people, and they were jumping out of their seats screaming, shouting, crying, and speaking in tongues. I thought to myself that they were so lucky and obviously "perfect." They must really know God and God must really love them. I felt like I was such a heathen, not worthy of God's love and attention.

Oh, how I longed to know God the way that they knew God. I was an absolute mess and how would I be able to do what they are doing? They didn't mess up like me, right?

The girls wore long skirts, blouses that covered everything, stockings, closed-toe shoes, and no make-up. I was the opposite.

Tammy Flowers-Hollis

My mother had spoken with the Pastor of the church, Bishop William J. Robinson, in advance and told him that she had a daughter that could sing. So, he called me to the front of the church to sing a solo during service. I was so amazed at the service and the support that was given to me mainly by the young people. They didn't act jealous. They were genuinely supporting me.

After the service, all the young people around my age gathered and just innocently fellowshipped. I sat in the cut just watching and waiting for my mother to say it was time to leave. I then noticed the crowd moving closer to me, and before I knew it, one of the girls looked at me with such a friendly, warm smile. She then said, "Hi, my name is Teresa and I go to Fashion Industries High School." I did not know how to take her smile or her friendliness. Who at the age of 16 is this friendly? Why is she so happy?

As I thought about those things, one of the many characters in my head decided to introduce itself, "Hi, I'm Tammy, and I go to LaGuardia." I said it with such cockiness as if to say I was in a better school and had a better life. She remained with a smile, unmoved. The other young people started to introduce themselves to me as well and then invited me to go with them to get pizza for lunch. I went to my mother to advise her of the same, thinking that she was going to say no, but quite the contrary. My mother became incredibly happy to see that I was going to be surrounded by God-Fearing young people and quickly went into her pocketbook and pulled out five dollars.

She further advised me to take my time and enjoy myself because we were going to stay for the afternoon service, too. I was okay with that, so I walked towards my new friends, and we all walked together laughing, joking, singing, and having clean fun.

We came back for the second service and then there was a night Bible study class called the YPWW (young people willing workers) and then by eight o'clock they were singing on the radio at night service. Wow, three services in a day together with Sunday school in the morning and YPWW. There wouldn't be any time to mess up because it felt like we lived in the church. However, I decided even with all the new life situations going on, I couldn't just turn my back on the streets.

Chapter 9

Can I Have My Cake & Eat It Too?

I remained the lookout for certain drug dealers, making sure they did not get caught selling the drugs or having too much money on them. That would make it obvious what they were doing. I began carrying weapons of all sorts to watch their backs. Thank God I never had to use them because the reality was no one ever taught me how to pull a trigger. I just figured it was scary enough for someone to know that I had it.

I eventually started dating a guy that was a part of the same cloth as me, so I thought; I liked him enough to be faithful. He allowed me to feel safe. Soon after, I introduced him to my mother, and I could tell he wasn't her favorite, but she didn't want to push me away, so she put on a front.

He had a huge pit bull, and he forced me to walk him so that the pit bull would become familiar with me. Scared out of my mind, knowing that if this dog wanted to rip me apart, there wouldn't be anything that he could do to stop him, but I did it.

One day while walking with him and this pit bull, a cat ran up a tree. I watched the dog jump over the fence and climb the tree to capture this cat. I thought to myself that wasn't a good thing. Just imagine if a human tried to get away and climbed on top of a car that means that this dog would jump on the car right after them, leaving no escape.

He introduced me to things I've never experienced before as well as some people that I would not have encountered on a normal day. This was exciting to me, and he came across as untouchable. I was really living life, and I walked with my head up high. I was seventeen years old and had made up my mind that if he wanted me to have his baby, I would. Even though I was still living with my mother when I woke up in the morning, he was there to say good morning and sometimes he would see me off to school. When I laid my head down at night, he was there to say good night, baby. Oh, how he loved me so. He knew that I had a curfew, so we tried to fulfill each day with our lust. I mean love.

I knew that I could trust him because he would always be with my older cousin, and I knew my cousin loved me enough that if anything went on behind my back, he would tell me. Further, what can he possibly do when he's always around me, right? One day I desired to stay out later than usual, and I conveyed that to him. I couldn't quite read him and his reaction.

It was something towards him becoming angry or very overprotective, whereas he really cared about my safety. I remember him saying that he didn't want me to be like the other chicks that had no respect for themselves but wanted me to remain "wholesome".

I chose to believe that he was just looking out for me, and I allowed him once again to capture me. Once he walked away, I began to go up the stairs to go into my apartment. My cousin followed me and called out to me. He then proceeded to tell me that this boyfriend is not being faithful and to stop trusting and believing all that he says. He further advised that the reason that my boyfriend was so in agreement with my curfew is it allowed him to be with other women openly.

I couldn't quite grasp this information to be true. How can this be? I spend so much time with him. I do everything that he asks me to do. I treat him better than I treat myself. I place him first. I love him. This simply cannot be true, but I thought even more about why my cousin would lie to me. He wouldn't!

I went upstairs and lay in my bed, and I could not close my eyes to sleep. I was truly trying to understand where I went wrong. But at the same time, I looked up towards the heavens for clarity. I knew that God was not pleased with me and that he had allowed me to know that this was not the right way to go, but my flesh drowned out his words to me.

The next morning when I awoke, my first thought was, I had to get a truthful answer from my boyfriend. I got up and dressed to meet him in front of the building. When I saw him, his face lit up as if he was so happy to see me. We then begin to walk hand in hand now and again glancing into each other's eyes. Eventually, we landed at his apartment he shared with his brother and cousin. We landed in his room, of course, in his bed.

Things began to become heated, and I was able to come to my senses and immediately placed my hand on his chest to push him away. "Are you faithful to me?" I asked.

"Of course, I am. Why would you ask me that? Don't you know that I love you and would never do anything to hurt you? I want to build a future with you, and you have my children." That was the kind of talk that would later have me in trouble. I believed him.

I found myself trying to bargain with God, asking him to make it doable for me to remain in the relationship with my boyfriend and somehow make it easier on me and the "saved thing." I would then try to combine my street life with my church life in hopes that all would mesh perfectly. I got closer to God mentally, but my flesh would remain weak.

Don't you understand, God, that this is hard? Life is hard, and he makes me happy! He loves me, God. Why are you making this so difficult for me? Haven't I been through enough? Ok, God, can I just have this one thing and everything else that you present to me I will obey you in? God, he's the best thing that is happening to me.

How can I serve you and you be happy with me, so I don't go to hell and at the same time allow me this one man? God, you are not here. You don't feel what I feel. You don't have to suffer like this. Well, no one is going to remain saved and be able to live like this. God, please!!!

I found myself in a constant struggle mentally, spiritually, and physically trying to compromise with God in hopes that he would change his rules for me. I have come up with my own rules to allow God to know what I am comfortable with so that he would meet me halfway. This may sound crazy, but that was my mindset. I was still seventeen years old and still living with my mother.

This night would be a night like no other. As I slept peacefully in my bed, I began to feel pain in my abdominal area. The pain became sharper as if someone was stabbing me. I was awake, holding onto my stomach. Still, the pain became so unbearable I rolled toward the edge of my bed and slid down slowly until I felt the floor. I was on my hands and knees, crawling to my mother's bedroom.

With tears in my eyes and all the wind I could gather, I cried to my mother, "Help, I'm in pain." My mother awoke and asked what I wanted her to do about it. I told my mother that I needed to go to the hospital. She looked at me and said, "Well, you need to find your way there because I am not taking you this time of morning." I pleaded with my mother to show compassion on me, but she remained stern.

I called for a cab and knew they wouldn't waste any time getting to me. The bad thing was I was in so much pain I couldn't dress myself. I decided to just go to the hospital in my pajamas. As everyone slept, I put my shoes on my feet and left the house. I tiptoed down the stairs, being all so careful not to drop down my feet to avoid more pain.

I was able to get into the cab and advised to be taken to Harlem Hospital, which was the closest hospital to where I lived. Harlem Hospital was well known for gunshot wounds, stabbing, and pneumonia. Yes, it was the same hospital that took care of my mother. After I paid the cab driver, I crawled out of his cab and into the hospital. They were used to so much real trauma that this didn't seem as serious. I was advised to just take a seat.

Finally, I was called into a room to see the doctor. The doctor examined me and said that they would need to run some tests. I just wanted the pain to disappear, so I told the doctor to do whatever he needed to do. At least an hour passed, and the doctor returned to the room. "So, doctor, what medication will you give me to stop this pain?"

And the doctor's response was, "Tammy, we can't allow you to leave. You will need to stay and receive treatment." I didn't quite understand what I was being told and why. The doctor then stated, "Tammy, you have contracted three sexually transmitted diseases at one time. If we do not begin treatment immediately, it can worsen and stop you from having children."

They then took me upstairs to a room where I would be separated from the world and everything, I thought I knew. How did I get not one disease but three? I've been faithful to him. What are these diseases, and will they stay with me for the rest of my life? I became so ashamed I would not allow myself to ask the doctor what all these diseases entailed. I figured that I should have known better. Shortly after, I was left alone in my room until a young lady entered. She asked me where I was from because I looked familiar. I told her I was from Edgecombe. We soon realized that we may not have known each other, but I knew her family, which was good enough.

We began to talk like we'd been friends forever. Telling jokes as we both tried to forget where we were and how we got there. She seemed truly knowledgeable about the streets and being free if you know what I mean. I felt uncomfortable, but I had to know, so I asked her, "What is PID?" She said that's when a man's penis is dirty, and if you have sex with him, all the bacteria from him transfer into you. I started to question, was my boyfriend's penis dirty? Was he not cleaning himself? This was absolutely disgusting to me. I started reflecting on my cousin and how he said my boyfriend was not faithful to me.

They released my hospital buddy the next day, and now I was back alone. I began to think about the many things that I had done wrong and asked myself what I was proving in what I was doing. I slowly started to realize that I was by myself. All the friends I thought I had were nowhere to be found.

Honestly, I didn't want them to be found because I would have to explain why I was in the hospital. As I lay in bed, I would try to sleep as much as possible, hoping the days would go by faster for me to be healed and released. However, whenever I opened my eyes, a nurse changed my medicine bag. So many drugs were being pumped into my system that it affected my breathing.

Sunday has now come, and normally I would go to church. I would attend Sunday school, morning service, afternoon service, and Young People Willing Worker's (YPWW) night service, whereas now I would sing on the radio every Sunday night with the choir and, many times, leading songs. But where am I? I am in the hospital because of my disobedience. I remember telling the Lord that I had learned my lesson and to show me how not to take that path again. A few Evangelists visited, and prayed, and encouraged me that Sunday. In my spirit, I felt unworthy of their prayer and time, but at the same time, I felt the power of the Holy Ghost fall on me. Everything I would do or say from there on out, I just wanted to be pleasing to God. They made me believe that there was hope for me yet. Once they left me, I would still pray to God and cry out without being ashamed. I started reading my Bible, hoping to get a life with God again.

I was in the hospital on Thanksgiving in 1994. My mother and her patient visited me with a huge plate of wonderful Thanksgiving food that my mother had cooked. She brought me a can of Juicy Juice as well. As she and her patient sat before me, I tried my best to swallow everything on that plate, but it did not quite work out. I had to get to the bathroom or there would be a mess all on the floor.

I barely reached the bathroom. All of what I had tried to eat came up, and there was such a smell. I asked my mother did she smelled what I smelled. She answered, "No." My mother then advised me that it was time for her to go and take care of me. We dared not show emotions, so I said a simple ok with a smile.

I continued vomiting throughout the night. I would ask everyone who would enter my room if they smelled what I smelled, but everyone looked at me as if I was crazy. I began placing toothpaste under my nose like a mustache to relieve myself, but nothing worked. I later found out that because of the constant medication pumped into my veins, the smell of the medication was coming through my pores. That's why I could not get away from it. The pain had drastically subsided, and the STDs were now gone. Thank God.

My doctor gave me a clean bill of health, and I was finally released from the hospital. I never felt so clear-minded and on fire for God. Sunday couldn't come fast enough for me. I wanted to be perfect in the sight of God and do everything right to show my appreciation. I stopped wearing pants and strictly stayed with long skirts or dresses. I covered up everything possible to turn the opposite sex away. I did not want to invite temptation my way.

Chapter 10

Clean Slate

Two weeks passed after being out of the hospital, and I decided to get my photo identification now with the DMV. I walked to 125th Street and got my first photo identification. This was the first time I could see my name on something that made me feel like I existed. I was so excited to have been accepted, "so to speak," and seeing positive movement in my life was a great feeling.

As I walked home feeling accomplished without hesitation, then suddenly, who popped up in front of me? The boyfriend that shared everything with me, including his diseases. He stood in front of me with a smile and excitement. He invited me to come with him to an apartment nearby, and, without hesitation, I did. We arrived in someone's room with a bed ready to be used, and it was my pleasure to sit in it. He didn't know he wouldn't get anywhere with me.

I wanted the space to chew him up and spit him out. He attempted to touch me, and I so kindly smacked his hand away. "Do you know that I was in the hospital?"

"Yes, I found out."

"But yet you did not come to visit me?"

"I just found out and was told you were being released."

"But I was in the hospital for two weeks. We would see each other every day; you mean to tell me that you didn't miss my presence sooner?"

"Baby, I'm just glad that you are home. I miss you so much."

"Really!!"

God had given me the strength to stand firm in my decision. I finally saw the truth and had a made-up mind not to waver. For the first time, I could place value on myself and knew that I deserved better. As I walked out of the room and eventually the apartment, I held my head up high and smiled with gratefulness to God in my heart. I was so grateful to feel God's presence and understood that only God was granting me strength and took the taste of that boyfriend from me.

Sunday couldn't come fast enough for me. I prepared my clothes the night before because I was so excited to get into the house of the Lord. I wanted to be around people that strived to be Christlike. I figured that would keep me on the right track. They then appointed me president of the youth choir called "The Anointed Voices," where I would now faithfully attend rehearsals and teach various songs.

I continued going to LaGuardia High School, where I was now singing in the gospel chorus. Not everyone was privy to taking that class. You had to be accepted as a bonus. I must say the gospel chorus was great. I was able to sing with a multitude of gospel talents. In contrast, many of those talented people are still relevant today. I learned there was more to singing than just sound.

Chapter 11

Where Did You Come From?

O ne day I was walking down the hallway in school and heard someone playing the piano in one of the music rooms. I walked into the room, and a young man approximately my age was sitting at the piano and, in musician's terms, making the piano talk. It had such a sound, and whoever played this piano had history. This could not be a student with all this soul and power.

He then began to sing a familiar song, assuming I would know it, and I did. As he sang, I took the top note. A huge smile pierced his face, and every tooth in his mouth came out of hiding. I must admit it pumped me. Before I knew it, LaSean was instructing me to try new vocals. He would say try this now, try it that way, and I understood him so well, to the point that he did not have to speak, and yet our talents would continue to communicate.

So, I asked LaSean where he came from because I had never seen him before. He simply said, "I'm here." That was good enough for me. LaSean and I would now sing and create music and songs every chance we got. After a while, LaSean had other students and me playing out the television show "Fame." We would walk down the halls singing harmony, creating with no limitations. Our vocals were absolutely crazy, and LaSean would somehow add fuel to the fire with his keys. LaSean and I became inseparable. Every chance we were able to join forces and create music, we grabbed it.

We no longer limited ourselves to school, but now we met at my house, church, and at Minisink Townhouse located in Harlem, New York. God had given LaSean a vision to form a community choir, and that's just what he did.

People would come out from various parts of the neighborhood and become one. LaSean would play the keys, and I would teach the vocals. We started accepting engagements in churches, neighborhood functions, and schools shortly afterward. We desired to encourage and uplift every spirit that we met.

Even though I would participate in all the festivities, I still fought for my life. Somehow, I would still find myself in the arms of a man, hoping to get it right this time. But I wouldn't get it right. It was very hard for me to be myself and to love myself.

I realized I was always seeking validation but did not understand why. Why did I believe that their happiness was more important than my own? I've placed myself in a dangerous position. At one time, I came close to slicing a man's hand open because he thought his hand was created to place fear in me. But I still stayed like a fool because, in the back of my mind, I tried to view him as I thought God would. However, the problem was that no one, including myself, had enough love and respect to feel that way toward me.

My old boyfriend had given me a few gold chains and a couple of rings, so when I met my new boyfriend, he stated that it was too dangerous for me to walk around wearing so much jewelry. He proposed that I let him hold my jewelry, and he would give me his gold chain to sport. At least it would only be one chain, and it would not bring too much attention to me, which in turn welcomed less danger, so he said.

I believed he was doing all of this in my best interest, so I agreed. As time passed, the longer I stayed with him, the more I became disgusted with myself because I knew that God had made me better than I was accepting. I felt like I dummied down to make him feel more confident.

One day, I was walking from a store near my aunt's apartment building and was stopped by a lady approximately three years older than me. I recognized her as residing in the same building as my aunt but was never formally introduced. She began to ask me questions.

Her first question was more like a statement, "You're Mattie's niece, right?"

I answered, "Yes."

"Do you know Dontae?"

"Yes."

"What is Dontae to you?"

"He is my boyfriend." I then asked why she was asking so many questions. She further advised me that she and Dontae had been together for years and that he lived with her. (That explained why his "grandmother" stayed sick and I couldn't go to his house).

She then asked me where he was, and I told her he was right on Edgecombe. She said, "Walk with me."

We started walking together towards the block, and as we drew closer, we could both see Dontae, and he could see us. Dontae then slid under a car to hide, but that wasn't the brightest move. His "real" girlfriend started fussing at him and told him to come to get his things out of her apartment. Earlier, she gave me her apartment number so I could come to her house if something happened.

Dontae walked with his "real" girlfriend back to the apartment, and I could hear him saying that I was a liar and he never had anything with me. I allowed them to go upstairs first, and when I finally reached the apartment, the door was wide open for me to just walk in. She was placing all his belongings in a black garbage bag. I could not find it within myself to get upset. I think because I was already at the point of being tired, used, and drained, the fight just wasn't worth it. I then told him I didn't care about his lies or even what was going on, I just wanted my jewelry back. He then said, "What jewelry?" I realized that I was never going to see my gold chains again. And I left, blaming myself for falling into the trap once again.

I went home, into my bedroom, and closed the door. I lay in my bed, looked up at the ceiling, and just stared as the tears ran down my face. As tears slid down my cheek to my neck and finally rested on my pillow I began to speak to the Lord. I told the Lord that I was so tired. I was tired of life and of the same ole pattern.

I felt I had done so much wrong that I wasn't worth His time and effort. I felt like I just couldn't get living for God right. At the same time, I was a liar, a punk, and a fighter. I had love but felt alone, embarrassed, and worthless. God, don't waste any more time on me. I could hear in my head that God was tired of me. I kept coming to Him, asking for forgiveness, and praying but kept messing up. I told God that so many other people can live better than me. So, God, I'm a loser. Let me go because I can't get any better. I felt like I was a lost cause.

I remembered making a deal with God that I would read my Bible every day and try my best to be perfect and at that time; I didn't understand the power of the flesh. I did not understand that I couldn't just read the Bible to say I read it, but I had to learn and understand how to apply it to my everyday life. More importantly, I did not know that this was a process.

That Sunday I went to church, and I was so discouraged and felt worthless in my spirit. I never conveyed my prayers or my thoughts to anyone. A mother in the church approached me and whispered in my ear, "God is not tired of you; he loves you and will not give up on you. That's the devil talking to you to discourage you. Don't give in to him."

I began crying because I realized the mother had to be right. How did she know about my conversation with God? How was she able to answer questions that I did not ask her? It had to have only been God. I lift my hands as the tears would stream down my face and begin to truly worship God in spirit and in truth.

I gathered more strength and encouragement to hold myself together for another week. I didn't quite have all the strength to stop all the wrongdoing in my life, but I had my mind made up to keep trying.

LaSean and I continued to minister in music and songs everywhere God allowed our feet to tread. LaSean soon became the musician for the Garden of Prayer, where he would play for all the choirs in the church and some of those choirs I would direct. Day by day we became increasingly like brother and sister. We fussed, fought, and argued. Life and the love of music would bring us right back together again.

Even though my life seemed quite chaotic at times, I continued attending school. I found myself balancing God, school, men, church, girlfriends, family, and the streets. There was a lot of good that I was experiencing in my life, but when the bad came, it hit hard.

I've witnessed so many deaths and senseless murders that it has become a way of life. I became numb to people dying. Going to jail was normal. Fighting was just something you had to do.

I remember there was a big-time drug dealer who sometimes would share his wealth. I didn't stop to think about how he obtained his finances or the many families he hurt by pushing the crack through the block. All I was able to see was the money. I didn't attempt to understand that he built his wealth on the death of others. I was selfish.

One day he disappeared, and no one had seen him for a while. Eventually, he turned up in a garbage bag chopped up in bits, and alongside him was another garbage bag which turned out to be his woman chopped up the same. Still, there was a little more to her. She was pregnant.

Shortly after those findings, gunshots erupted around the block again, and now it was another drug dealer. Someone used a shotgun and blew his head straight from his body. His body dropped into the street near a curb, but his head rolled under a truck. As I walked past him, all I could see was a navy-blue bubble coat with shoulders, arms, and hands, but the head was definitely gone.

I remember becoming very angry because the cop just stood there waiting for the coroner. I asked him to at least place a sheet over the victim and his response was, "What for? All you see is the coat." This was being said as the drug dealer's blood traced the fallen white snow. I further asked the officer, "How long will you guys have him just laying here?"

And the officer's response was, "What's the rush his body is on ice."

Even though I had become numb, I couldn't help wondering what kind of world I lived in. I kept going to school, but there were plenty of days I decided not to go. Not because I was sad or depressed, but I thought cutting school was not that big of a deal.

Chapter 12

The Last One

While I would attend school now on my own terms, I began to pick up foul habits. I had sticky fingers. My mother was proud of me as I was in my senior year of high school. I told her the cost of the yearbook (that I was never in) and the cap and gown. She gladly provided me with those funds that were supposed to be paid to the school and I spent it. I figured I had more than enough time to gather another one hundred dollars before the last payment date was due.

One day, my mother instructed me to go to the bank for her to get some funds out of the ATM. I walked up the hill to the bank and somehow thought I was smarter than my mother. Boy, I was wrong. After printing out the starting balance, I withdrew the amount she requested. I then printed out the ending balance and the receipts I would provide to my mother.

Unfortunately, I went a bit further and withdrew another one hundred dollars to cover myself with the one hundred dollars my mother initially gave me for my high school items.

I came home and gave my mother what she instructed me. I went into my bedroom and hid the stolen money in one of my encyclopedias. As time passed, I forgot where I had hidden the one hundred dollars. I was screwed. How was I going to pay for the cap and gown? I didn't even care about the yearbook at this point. What tickets would I provide to my mother to watch me walk down the aisle come graduation time?

WAIT!!!! I'm not even graduating because they advised me, I failed a test, which prevented me from graduating. How can I tell my mother this? How can I tell the church folks this? They also gave me money to graduate. My mother had already invited my god brother as her plus one. No money, tickets, graduation cap and gown, and NO DIPLOMA.

Time drew near for me to "graduate," and I would hear my mother bragging proudly about how I made it. I couldn't bear to see my mother be embarrassed for my wrongdoings and I was not going to see my mother hurt. I couldn't come to tell her I had screwed up again.

Graduation day is here, and my mother asked what happened to the tickets. I told her that I was going to the school early to pick them up.

She thought nothing strange about it, so I was good at that. When I closed my mother's apartment door, I started praying to God. I cried out loud to God as I walked up the Jamaican hill to the train station. Once I got on the train, I kept praying and believing that God was going to come through. I no longer cared about myself and how people possibly were viewing me. This was about me not letting my mother down.

CIRCLES

I prayed to God and asked him to rescue me for my mother's sake. If I never cared about people's thoughts or feelings about me and whether I was crazy, this was the day. There was nothing or nobody that I was going to allow to distract me. I was on a mission. (Isn't that how we ought to be when we call ourselves children of God? We are supposed to be about our father's business. Allowing no distractions but standing firm with a made-up mind that for God I live and for God I die.)

I finally made it to the school and went upstairs into an office only to see a box of caps and gowns through a hard plastic window locked behind a big, solid wooden door. So many thoughts played in my mind on how to retrieve that box. Was I bold enough to bust the window out of the door? But if I do that, who will lift me through the window? What if I get stuck? Or worse, what if I get caught?

"I began to give up and face the reality that I messed up, and it wasn't fair to place God in that position to help me. God, here it is any other time I go about my business doing what I want to do. I don't even acknowledge you as I should, but now I have the nerve to ask for your help. It's not fair to you, God, and all I am doing right now is using you when here it is, you've been so good to me, and I still gave you my back. God, I'm just going to come clean. How bad can the punishment be? I rather make you proud of me God, for being honest rather than continuing to lie."

This was my talk with God as I walked from my school to where the graduation was to be held. Walking through the lobby, I did not see my mother or godbrother. I continued up the stairs. I mean, what was I doing all of this for? I was not going to receive a diploma. They would not call my name as I walked across the stage. Suddenly, I saw a box on the floor and inside that box I could see caps and gowns that people were pulling out. I went to the box and retrieved the very last cap and gown. I placed it on and walked into the auditorium; the graduates' last rows were not full, so I could sit down. There were programs rolled up with a red ribbon tied around it and I got one. The ceremony was ending, and I was just there. After they saluted all the graduates, I came out of the auditorium and there stood my mother and my god brother. I looked at her and said, "How did you get in?" My mother said thank God there was a lady downstairs who said she had an extra ticket and somehow, they stumbled across one more for my god brother. So, I just looked at her, not desiring to tell the truth but to shut up.

My mother said," I didn't see you walk across the stage. I guess I got upstairs too late." I don't remember responding to my mother concerning that statement, but I encouraged her to move on from it.

We got back on the train after walking from the graduation site. I was not happy about deceiving my mother, but I was ecstatic about seeing the movement of God. I understood nothing happens by coincidence, but everything was strategically placed in an order and God had set that up.

Once we arrived around the block, my mother took me to my elementary school just across the street from the house and stood me in front of the office. She was so proud and wanted to allow those that couldn't see me succeeding in life to see me in my cap and gown and to know that I had made it. I stood proud with my head lifted and a smile from ear to ear on my face. No, I was not worthy of this, but my mother was! I could not take that away from my mother.

After "*graduating*," it was now time to get a job and figure out what was next.

Chapter 13

❧

Who's That?

In the year of 1995, LaSean became the music teacher at P.S. 194 Countee Cullen Elementary School in Harlem, New York. He invited me to contribute to the vocal teachings of his students. I continued for the next year working at cafes and singing with LaSean. I would remain with him until nightfall and all the students would be gone. We would just be two creative minds coming together to see what's next.

The school year was over, and we entered the summer where LaSean and I would continue teaching the elementary school children, but now on a summer schedule. One evening LaSean and I sat at his piano and began to brainstorm. As I started singing, I saw a security guard enter the auditorium. I thought he was coming in to advise LaSean and me we had to leave simply because we would always lose track of time. However, that was not his objective. He came in to listen to the music.

I found him to be attractive, and his smile had me. The flirting began because I wanted to know more about him. I started going to the elementary school almost daily, hoping to see him. Eventually, I asked if he had a girlfriend and he answered no. He then asked me if I had a boyfriend, and my answer was no. We both smiled, and he asked me out on a date.

The date he took me on did not consist of fancy restaurants or dressy clothes, but of a pizza shop on the back of his bike.

He picked me up from my house and we rode his bike for approximately an hour to the pizza shop. Can you imagine being a female sitting on a hard seat for almost an hour? I felt every bump made known to mankind (smile). When we finally made it to the pizza shop, he held the bike up so that I wouldn't fall climbing down. As I slowly slid down the side of his bike, I realized within that time I became bowlegged. It was difficult for me to stand straight, but I faked the funk and kept it moving.

I was introduced to the biggest slice of pizza I had ever seen and eaten. We had an awesome time and afterward, we walked to his neighborhood park. I sat on the swing as he stood up against the gate and just talked about life and where we see ourselves in the years to come. I was nervous, yet I was comfortable about being around him.

We later walked back to my house, and it seemed like it was a shorter walk compared to riding his bike. I guess because it was less painful, and we really had a lot to share.

We would spend a lot of moments with each other building on something neither one had ever had, which was true love and friendship. Eventually, I introduced him to my mother; her response was a simple smile. As if to say, *I wonder how long this one will last.*

He and I spent every chance possible with each other. He was different from my norm. He wasn't concerned about my body, but my thoughts and well-being. I remember making moves on him to entice him into having sex and he would show that there was so much more to do rather than to have sex. I was very intrigued by that. It was about that time we made our relationship official.

I received a phone call from a sister in the church requesting my presence. I didn't quite understand why, but I went. When I arrived at the church, I witnessed one of the sisters in the church singing a song I wasn't quite used to hearing her sing. It was what we called a "street" song. I saw two men sitting there, but why? Up next, there was a gentleman that could bring the beast out of a choir and tame it. I looked up to him and respected everything about him, but why was he now singing a street song, too?

Now, it was my turn, and they asked me to sing a song as the infamous Richard Tolbert Sr. would play. So, I sang "His Eye Is on the Sparrow" and the two gentlemen sat in amazement and afterward clapped as if I gave them a personal show. "Why am I singing?" I asked. "Well, these two gentlemen are producers and have produced many great people."

"Oh, so this was an audition?"

"Yes, and we like you. We want you BUT you cannot say Jesus or God!!!"

How can I sing gospel and not incorporate those names? Then it wouldn't be gospel. I gave a solid, "No."

Mr. Tolbert Sr. pulled me into the kitchen and told me how proud he was of my decision and that God was pleased with my response. He told me to hold on because God would bless me with more. Of course, this reassured me that I was making the right decision. I stood for him.

That Sunday, my Pastor William J. Robinson called me up to the front of the church and presented me with flowers to say how proud he was of me as well. I was so overjoyed that I made the right decision, and I did not doubt that God was also pleased. It was like being the opposite of Peter when he denied Christ. I stood proud and unashamed to represent God, even though I knew that more work would be done in me.

Two weeks later, on a Tuesday, I went to a Mass Choir rehearsal where my pastor taught the songs that night. Toward the end of the rehearsal, my pastor stated, "Tammy Flowers will be singing at the Apollo Theatre on 125th Street." I looked around trying to see if there was another Tammy Flowers because I had not signed up for Apollo. Everyone began looking at me and saying congratulations. I told them I never signed up for Apollo and my pastor advised that he signed me up.

Before I knew it, time had passed, and it was now time to go to the Apollo. I walked in, not knowing what to expect. I did not have to audition because I was scheduled for gospel night. I stood on the infamous Apollo Theater stage and did a quick run through with the musicians that would play for me.

God had granted favor right then and there. I do not remember her name but realized she saw greatness in me. As I was singing, I saw the tears come to her eyes, and not too long afterward; she told me to stop and save my vocals for the show. She placed such a smile on her face as if I was her child, making a mother proud.

That night, my church family and my bloodline showed up to support me. It was such an amazing night, and I was able to win fourth place. I was satisfied with that. I thought that was all for the show. You either win or lose and then go home, but then I was advised that I would need to continue. I competed against singers of all genres, dancers, rappers, magicians, and whatever else that would be presented on stage.

I did not argue but accepted the challenge. A few months had passed, and it was time to go on stage again. I tried to remain humble and kept telling myself I was not there for a show but to minister. My ministering would be worth it if I could reach just one person.

I walked out onto the stage and rubbed the wood for "good luck," even though I didn't believe in luck. Doug E Fresh introduced me to the audience after I spoke briefly with him. I wanted to change the song that I previously sung but was advised not to. So, that meant that I had to present this song to the audience as if they had never heard it before. I walked toward the middle of the stage and stood still. The spotlight not only shined oh so brightly, but I could also feel the heat from the light. I started singing, "His Eye Is On The Sparrow" and the crowd started to boo me.

I was here not to become friends, not to know or understand my audience, but to minister. Suddenly, I heard a loud voice on the right side of me from the balcony say, "Sing Baby Sing." My Pastor, Bishop William J. Robinson, and Dorothy Black, better known as "Mother Black," were cheering me on. I then began to feel strength and refused defeat.

God had given me this moment not to shine, but for him to shine through me. This was bigger than me and I realized that. If God was for me, who could be against me? No one or nothing could stop me or block me on that night. I could complete my song without "Sandman" coming out on the stage and kicking me off.

Once all the performers were finished, we returned to the stage to see who the winners would be. Doug E Fresh placed his hand over each of us one at a time, as the crowd would judge. There was a trio that sang that night, and they were children.

The girl was about 10 years old, and she sang tenor. Her ridiculously small twin brother stood in the middle singing soprano. And lastly, the other brother sang alto. They were so amazing I stood up and clapped for them as well. Needless to say, they won first place. I did not see competition, just ministry.

Doug E Fresh was coming back around for the second time and all of a sudden, the audience became louder and louder. Before I knew it, the Apollo as a whole stood up and chanted my name, "Tammy, Tammy, Tammy."

Everywhere I looked, I could see people of all colors, shapes, and sizes on their feet as their arms would wave in the air, chanting my name louder and louder.

I was instructed to walk forward so that I would be able to show the audience that they were being heard and that I accepted the second-place position. And my boyfriend stood right in the front as if he was directing a choir waving his arms in the air and chanting the same, or even louder. Yes, indeed, that was a night to remember!

Chapter 14

God, This One Is For You

On December 25, 1995, my boyfriend proposed to me and even though it was exciting, there was somewhat of an off feeling. Was I too young for this? Was I moving too fast? But there was a thought that threw all those doubts out of the way. I was raised and taught that God honors marriage. I understood that first came love, marriage, and then the baby in a baby's carriage. I wanted to honor God and follow what I believed to be the right way. So, I said, *"Yes."*

I went and showed my mother the ring. I thought she would add some enthusiasm to this "joyous" occasion, but she didn't. My mother did not want to come across as if she wasn't happy for me, but she couldn't shake the feeling that something was wrong.

My fiancé and I continued dating. Now he was comfortable enough to introduce me to his mother, father, brothers, aunts, cousins, and female best friend. We aimed to become more of an item and let people know we planned to stay together. We went to various family functions on my side and his together. His mother knew I was a singer, so she invited me to her church. I didn't mind, even though I could tell she wasn't too fond of me. Shortly afterward, I sang for events, concerts, and anniversaries at her church.

I went back to my mother after speaking with my future husband and let her know that we were scheduled to get married on September 7, 1996. My mother then sat me down and asked if I was pregnant, and my answer was "No." She then asked, "Why are you getting married? If you are pregnant, just know that I am saying that you do not have to get married." One of her famous sayings is "You are not the first and you sholе won't be the last." That's her way of saying if I made a mistake, it will still be alright. However, I confirmed once more that I wasn't pregnant.

Unfortunately, I couldn't say that I was doing it for love either, but the focus was I wanted to be pleasing to God. I felt like this was a way to make up for all my screw ups and promiscuities.

I could see then that my mother was hurt but did not want to interfere with "my" life. So, instead of her badgering me to make me feel bad, she jumped on the bandwagon. She found a way to contribute to my wedding and reception, making it a success. My mother purchased all the meat and more. My Aunt Mattie, who took us in when we first moved to New York, cooked a lot of the food.

We had a brother named Paul, and he oversaw maintaining the appearance and cleanliness of the church, and he absolutely did just that. The mothers in the church pitched in as well with their sleeves rolled up and aprons covering their dresses. I watched as they stood in front of the church kitchen sink to clean and season the chicken.

The wedding day was approaching quickly, with much to be done. My husband-to-be and I came to an agreement that the colors were going to be baby blue and white. He chose two of his best friends to be his best men, and I chose two friends who were more like sisters to me.

It was time to find my sisters their bridal dresses and so we traveled all around the streets of New York looking at the best dresses New York had to offer, of course within a reasonable price range. We had so much fun bonding and eating within that day and the experience overjoyed me. Eventually, we found two beautiful baby blue dresses that were perfect on both.

Now it was my turn to locate my wedding gown. My god brother Logan told me he would purchase my wedding gown, so he and I went looking. We went to David's Bridal, and I began to try on wedding gowns. It was amazingly fun considering I was shopping with my god brother and not many women. But I must admit that he had an eye for style.

After trying on so many wedding gowns, we finally found the one. It was pretty and only ninety-nine dollars. Yes, this made him happy to know that this dress would not break his pockets.

So, my god brother paid for the gown, and we headed back home to show it off to my mother. She seemingly liked it. The big day was approaching fast, and we needed a place to live. We were able to obtain a one-bedroom apartment in Harlem on Sugar Hill. This was just up the hill from my mother's apartment. Great start, I thought, because God was allowing all of this to happen for us. God must be pleased, right?

As time passed, I realized that I did not have a father to walk me down the aisle. I wasn't bothered by that. I was used to not having him around. It seemed natural. Besides, I still had my oldest brother and my uncles. I chose my oldest brother.

A few weeks before the wedding, I received a phone call from my father. Oh, what a surprise he was calling me from prison. I wanted to keep peace, especially because my mother was still living in the same apartment building before, he had left, and I did not want to trigger anything. We were used to him being in jail and getting in and out as if that were normal. We just weren't sure how long he would be in this time.

I answered the phone and after hearing which prison he was in at this time I said, "Hi Daddy." His response would always be, "How's daddy's baby? You know that nobody better not touch my daughter. I will kill somebody if they touch my daughter." And the conversation would continue with me convincing him that I'm good and so are my brothers and that another man has not replaced him in our lives.

I asked my father when he would be getting out and it sounded like it was going to be awhile, so I was okay with letting him know that I was getting married. I asked, just to make sure that he would not be able to make it. He told me that he would send money to help with the expenses

CIRCLES

and that he was sorry for not being able to make it. I didn't believe him and honestly; I did not care.

September 6, 1996, had arrived, and we all went to the church to decorate. All invitations were given out and answered, food was being prepared and everything was going according to plan. I stayed at my aunt's house for the night because my bridesmaids would meet me there in the morning to get ready for the big day.

Meanwhile, my husband-to-be worked towards gathering his best men. One was in New York and the other was away at school. On the day of the wedding, he was advised that there was a great big snowstorm and that his best friend that was away at school was not going to be able to make it.

I received the news and began to get a bit nervous. Was this a sign? My aunt and my bridesmaids encouraged me not to worry and that everything would work out fine. We soon concluded that the bridesmaids would need to walk down the aisle by themselves, and when the ceremony was over, they then stood on each side of the best man and walk out.

Chapter 15

What Did I Do?

On September 7, 1996, I married Mister. We enjoyed the day, the food, the attention, the love shown by family and friends, and the many gifts. Once the reception was over, I realized I was no longer going home with my mother but with a man. I could no longer play around with my brothers and sister, but now I had to become a grown-up. Everyone was counting on me, right?

I finally reached the apartment set up for me and Mister to live in. Reality started to set in. My father-in-law walked into the apartment with our wedding gifts, and I remember such sadness came over me. Was this not supposed to be a joyful day? Shouldn't I feel a sense of excitement? I mean, this is a new and better chapter in my life, right?

I began to talk myself into being happy for this "special occasion." It was time to grow up!! I was nineteen and in one month, the word teen would no longer be attached to my age.

So, now the gifts started to rack up, and I became excited about opening them. I waited for Mister to come upstairs to open them together. He finally came upstairs, and I immediately said, "Let's wait to lie down. I want to open the gifts first." As we began opening the gifts, I started feeling like I was a real grown-up. I was now going to make decisions pertaining to my household and family, like decorating, food to cook, detergent to use to wash clothes, etc.

Now it was time to open the envelopes, which meant money. We both agreed to open a bank account with both of our names on it and those funds were to be used to service us in life and on the honeymoon to Atlantic City in New Jersey. We stayed at the Clarion Hotel and ate at all the All-U-Can-Eat-Buffets for the entire stay. We walked the Boardwalk hand in hand, doing pretty much anything that was cheap or free. I didn't have high expectations. I never set goals for myself. There was no blueprint in place for me to follow. I just hoped that all would be well because this was supposed to be our world. But I did notice something on my honeymoon. He was cheap, controlling, and did I mention cheap?

Eventually, we made it back to New York City and boy was I glad. I couldn't wait to see my mom, brothers, and my little sister. Being around my mom gave me a sense of peace. I started desiring to rewind and change my mind about the huge choice I had made.

Home sweet home. Wait, Tammy, this was no longer your home. Your home was up the hill inside a brownstone. Remember, you live on the 2nd floor. Oh, yeah!!!

As I tried to perform my wifely duties and wait for the love in me to reveal itself to me for my husband, we began to have family gatherings. I told everyone that I was going to make fresh collard greens. I never really knew how to cook then, but now I was going to start.

This was a big deal because this would be the first dinner party that we would give as a married couple. So, I purchased the greens and was told I would need to wash them well. No one had explained to me how to wash the greens. I placed the greens on the coffee table in my living room and then I stepped out of the living room briefly. When I came back, I found all kinds of bugs crawling on my coffee table. I was so disgusted that I took the greens and placed them into my kitchen sink, poured Dawn dish detergent, and washed them as if they were clothes. I rinsed the greens and placed them in a pot with smoked neck bones, as per instructed by my mother (the very one who doesn't like collard greens).

Our family and friends started to show up and bring their dishes to the table. Meanwhile, in the kitchen, I was no longer cooking greens but bubbles. My cousin asked, "What are you cooking?" I proudly said, "Collard greens." She gave me such a look and said, "Collard greens don't have bubbles."

So, I dust the bubbles off, poured out the water, and placed fresh water in the pot. But the bubbles kept coming back.

Needless to say, no one had a taste for collard greens that night. My mom stayed home but sent word to just send her a plate of white rice. She was not going to take the chance on my cooking.

I enjoyed myself that night being surrounded by other people. Not feeling like I'm separated from the world, and it took me back to more happy times in my life where I felt free and was able to be Tammy.

I was tired of feeling by myself and I wanted something to love. Remember, at the age of 17, I was advised that I wouldn't be able to have children because of a life of promiscuity and diseases. I decided to fight against those odds. I may not have been perfect, but I knew God and that he was able to do the impossible. So, Mister and I prayed that night that God would open my womb and allow me to conceive. We placed our faith in God and tried not to think about it any further.

A few weeks passed and Mister and I were in the bedroom having a conversation and before I knew it, anger had risen in him. Could it be that I had an opinion that differed from his? Could it be that I was becoming too smart for my own good? Or could it be that another gentleman was being too nice to me? Before I knew it, he charged at me in the bedroom and rammed his head into my stomach. I and my one hundred pounds went flying across the bed. I did not know what to think because this was new. How do I respond to this? I must show this man that I can be just as crazy. But Tammy, you are not crazy. What if your plan backfired and this man killed you in here? Ok, well, I must see how he responds.

I had made myself a hot cup of tea a few moments before. I picked it up and aimed for the wall but wanted him to believe I meant to hit him. He remained unbothered as the tea flew over my wall and lamp. I knew from there that I would be in trouble. However, that day he did not continue the physical abuse. I received a call from the Apollo. I was reminded that I had won three times and had the opportunity to win the fourth, which would allow me to obtain a record deal, but I stated that I recently became married and wanted to take a breather.

A few months later, I started all over and was okay with that. It was now my fifth time going on the stage to continue this competition, but something felt different. I was feeling different. I was hungry this particular day, so I went to KFC and ordered a three-piece chicken meal with mashed potatoes and gravy, coleslaw, extra biscuits, a huge Pepsi, and a chocolate cake. I sat in my dressing room and looked at myself in the mirror as I would eat all this food.

I just couldn't help myself and now it was time for me to go out on that stage and I felt like I was rolling out there instead of walking. I remember speaking a word of prayer to God, asking him to let me win but, in my heart, I didn't want to. I did not like to compete.

When I finished struggling to sing, losing did not surprise or sadden me, but I was relieved. When I stepped outside to meet my mother and my aunt, my aunt said to my mother, "Debra, didn't Tammy look a bit fat up there singing?" My mother said she didn't notice, so we moved on from that conversation.

A few months passed, and I felt nauseous and bloated, and Aunt Flow was MIA. I went to the doctor and received the best news ever. I told my mom that I believed that I was pregnant. She said, "I know better than that!" I soon needed to remind my mom that I was a grownup and married.

"Tammy, you're pregnant." I was so excited and just wanted to share it with the world. Now, this would give Mister a reason not to abuse me. This is his child within me; I'm sure he would love this baby like I do. There's no way this man would harm me knowing that he can hurt his child inside me, right? I began to receive a lot of attention from the people in the church, our family and friends, and he did not like that. I began to feel stronger in my walk with God and alive. I would sing until the heavens would open and I would feel God's hands on my face. The more stronger I became in my faith, the more the enemy attacked.

God had now blessed us to move from Manhattan to the South Bronx into a bigger apartment. I was so excited about movement and to know that my baby would have space to run, crawl, and enjoy life. It wasn't about me but about my baby's happiness.

Chapter 16

Do I Matter?

I was just so excited that life was going in the correct order for me. Mister and I attended Lamaze classes and read books on how the baby was growing and what to look forward to during the birthing process. We did not want to know the sex of the baby. We figured that it would bring more excitement to find out in the moment.

Everyone was so happy for us. I would hear how beautiful I looked and how my hair was growing. I was told that I stayed with a glow around me. Good things and good people encouraged me throughout my pregnancy. Yes, this was to be a great time in our life. Unfortunately, that was not always the case.

I was approximately 5 months when Mister and I started walking up a steep hill that connected us to our new Bronx apartment. At this time, we did not have a car, so we would sometimes take a bus home from church. I wore a yellow dress, off-white stockings, and brown dress flats this day (This is what comes to mind whenever I remember this moment).

As we moved closer to the top of the hill, I remember Mister becoming angry. I do not know what triggered his anger this time, but I can tell you what happened next. There was no ice or a smooth wooden floor, and no music playing, but I found myself quickly skating down the hill in my brown dress flats. Instead of falling, my shoes rode it out until I reached the bottom of the hill. Maybe it was something I said, or how I may have looked, but the green-eyed monster returned.

As I walked back up the hill, I was simply at a loss for words. I couldn't grasp that he pushed me down the hill while pregnant. God was and is so good, I never fell. Maybe I had the first pair of skate shoes because I glided easily. I tried to understand what had just happened. My heart was broken, and I became embarrassed and ashamed, hoping no one was able to witness this "quarrel." I held my head low and continued up the hill. I kept my mouth shut as the tears streamed down my face.

I felt a sense of childlike fear, which made me quiet, nervous, heartbroken, and humble. Maybe I said something wrong. Maybe I deserved this. I knew that no matter the answer, I could not tell my mother. She would more likely remind me that she warned me.

It was too early in the marriage to show that I made a bad decision. I'd keep this secret to myself.

Once we arrived upstairs, he apologized and said he would never do it again. I wanted to believe him not because of love, but because I had nowhere else to go. There would be weeks that would pass. Sometimes days would pass without abuse. But each time it occurred; it would become worse. At times, there would be such jealousy because a male looked at me or spoke to me, not necessarily flirting but I would be punished for those things.

At seven and a half months pregnant with our first baby, I lay in our bed. Mister called it playing. But of course, we knew that was not true. He climbed upon my pregnant belly and sat down, all two hundred pounds of him. He lifted both of my arms and made his way to each wrist. In doing so, he now had complete control of me. He jerked my wrist back and forth, forcing me to slap myself. Before I knew it my hand had hit my left eye. He repeated this act until the blood vessel in my eye burst.

Eventually, he climbed down and walked away as if to say it was not that serious. Somehow in his mind, it was not his fault, and it was simply a mistake.

As time passed on, he found himself "playing" once again. This time he had a pair of nun chucks and as I would lie in the bed once again pregnant, he took the nun chucks and pretended to be Bruce Lee. As he stood at the foot of the bed, he swung the nun chucks in every way possible until they landed extremely hard on my feet. My feet had swelled more than two times the original size. I was unable to walk and unable to put my footwear on. I heard sorry once again!

I stayed because I was embarrassed and ashamed. Many people, especially from the streets, understood that I was tough and never to be a pushover. How would I look to allow people to know that I was now weak?

I learned how to master putting on a smile while being broken, embarrassed, discouraged, and just flat-out hurt. When I was about eight months or so, I went into the bathroom to shower, and Mister was in the bathroom as well. He was placing curls in his hair using a kit. This kit had lye in it, which is the same key ingredient as a relaxer.

Mister became upset once again. Maybe because I wanted to take a shower while he was working on his hair. I really do not know, but as I attempted to get into the bathtub, he pushed me, and I quickly grabbed hold of the shower curtain and reached for the shower rod. I held on for dear life so that my belly wouldn't hit the knobs that protruded from the wall.

I was able to stand firm enough to climb out of the tub. At the same time, I became enraged and scared. I grabbed a hand full of the cream in the kit that contained lye chemical and even though I did not have long fingernails; I scratched his arm to the best of my ability. I followed the scratch by rubbing the cream from the kit on it. I did not know how it would turn out from there, but I had to try.

Mister let out a loud scream. He was in pain and tried to wash it off. Before I knew it, he had threatened to harm himself. He climbed out the window and stood on the fire escape.

I then hurried and closed him outside on the fire escape, not caring if he would take his life. I then heard the Holy Spirit remind me that his death would be on my hand, and I didn't want that. I reluctantly opened up the window so he could choose when he wanted to return inside.

When he did come back inside, he asked me if I cared what happened to him and my heart had hardened so much. My answer was NO!

We continued to live and have some good days and some bad days. Through it all, I couldn't complain because my faith allowed me to know that God would never leave me and that it was going to work out all in due time.

It was now close to the time of me having my baby, but I couldn't stay home by myself. Mister and I went to stay with my mother. On November 2, 1997, at about 3:00 am, I started having pain in my abdominal area. I have felt this pain before, but instead of the pain leaving, it stayed for a while. Every five minutes, I would feel this tightening in my stomach. I got out of bed and walked to my mother's bedroom. My mother was told by me that I was in labor, and my contractions were five minutes apart.

She then stated that I would still have a while to go, so try to go and rest. I took heed and I tried. The pain was still there, but it was not unbearable. That Sunday morning came with full force, and I was still going. My mother advised Mister that it would be alright for him to go to church, and she would stay with me. He agreed.

As time passed, I started feeling a bit damp. I knew that I hadn't used the bathroom on myself, but what was this? I told my mother, and she immediately made me get off her couch. She said, "Your water bag is leaking." She then retrieved about five plastic bags and lined her couch with them. After she felt her couch was fully secured, she then permitted me to sit down.

Enough time had passed now, and I was feeling the pain. I felt like there weren't any breaks to breathe. I went to my mother and in the deepest voice that I could speak.

CIRCLES

"I am sure that I am ready to go NOW!" I shouted. My mother called the ambulance, and they came quickly.

She told Mister to meet us at the hospital as she and her best friend rode with me in the ambulance. By the time I had arrived at the hospital, I dilated seven and a half centimeters.

My mother yelled to the top of her lungs, "We gonna have a baby." She was so excited. I mean, think about it, this was going to be her first grandchild. Mister made it to the hospital while I remained in labor.

Now it was time to push, and something dawned on me. "Come here doctor, I just realized something."

The doctor asked, "What is that?"

I then responded and said, "Nothing can come out of there, I'm too small." The doctor then chuckled and went back to what he was doing.

Finally, after nineteen hours of labor, we had a baby girl. I didn't see her immediately, but my mom, my mom's best friend, her father, and her godmother laid eyes on her first.

All I could see from a distance was a lot of hair. Not just on her head, but also on her back and arms. What was this that I pushed out? Was she a werewolf? No, she was perfect, and she was all mine.

We named her after us as the parents and both of her grandmothers. Yes, this was a really great time in my life. All that I had suffered from, she made it all worthwhile.

I went back to my mother's house because, of course, my baby girl was my first baby and even though I read books and have been schooled by many mothers, I was sure I needed her. She taught me how to breastfeed, clean my baby properly, use various positions to burp my baby and so much more. Not to mention whenever I needed a break, she was right there.

Mister and I agreed on making Teresa her godmother. Teresa was the one that I met at 16 years old in the church and she approached me with the biggest smile just to say *hi*. Teresa didn't take her role lightly. She immediately rolled up her sleeves and went to work.

I stayed with my mother for about one month and was told by my husband that it was now time to come home (sounds familiar?) I did not want to go home. The love and peace of mind that I was receiving was very much needed. I knew I could not stay with my mother forever, so I mustered up enough courage to return home.

Mister was jealous of the attention I was giving to our daughter. I didn't feel good about lying back down anymore because I wanted to make sure that every part of me was pure for her. I realized that I was no longer focused on our relationship, but everything revolved around our daughter.

Before I knew it, our daughter was now three months old. Mister invited a childhood friend over to the house to meet our daughter. This childhood friend was and is a well-known actor, so it was obvious that Mister wanted to show off his accomplishments. There was a knock at the door, and I could see the excitement in Mister's eyes. I stood in the doorway of our bedroom, excited for my husband. I did not need to dress up, so I kept wearing my old red flowered robe with torn hanging pockets that my mother had passed down to me.

He opened the door, and a smile came across his face. He welcomed his friend to our humbled abode and led him into the living room. He summoned me to bring our daughter to the living room shortly afterward. As she lay in her bassinet, I pushed her toward the living room with a simple smile. I was not star-struck but simply happy to see that my husband was excited to show off his family. He introduced me and just as quickly as he stated my title "wife," he dismissed me back to the bedroom and told me to leave our daughter with him.

I left the living room feeling embarrassed, ashamed, and simply not worthy of being in the company of adults. Furthermore, I had never separated from my daughter before, so this task was not easy, to say the least. Before this day, I had never allowed a man other than her father to touch her and definitely not hold her. So many painful thoughts ran through my mind, but I had to trust God and believe that he would protect my baby girl.

Finally, my sweet baby was back in my arms. I was not allowed to leave the bedroom, so I had to wait for Mister to bring her back to me.

Wow, an entire month passed, and my perfect angel was now four months old. This didn't mean that life was easy. I just learned how to exist, not live. We had not too long come back home from church.

As I removed my dress and wore a pink slip, I looked at our daughter laying quietly in her bassinet. I felt sad for her and yet angry at myself because of the life I forced her to live. This was not fair to her. I didn't care about myself, but she was my everything. The many fights and arguments she have witnessed. I was supposed to protect her. She shouldn't have to suffer with me. These were a few of my thoughts.

Mister was yelling as usual. I realized that he was threatening violence from the kitchen, which was a little way off from the bedroom. The wheels in my head began to turn. I thought to myself that this would be the best time to run and take my baby with me. I gently picked my baby up and held her tightly to my bosom. Then I slowly walked towards the door, ensuring not to alarm Mister of my soon-to-be freedom.

The adrenaline was pumping through my veins. I couldn't turn back now. It was now or never. I quickly turned the lock and swung the door wide open. I ran as fast as I possibly could, however, it was difficult because I was carrying extra weight. I thought to myself, If I could just make it to Sister Della's house. Sister Della went to the same church as us and she lived on the fourth floor. We lived on the sixth floor. I knew that if I could make it close enough to knock on Sister Della's door. My baby and I would be safe.

Sadly, he caught me by my hair and dragged me back into the apartment as I continued to hold our baby to my bosom. I didn't know what punishment was coming, but I knew that it was going to be bad. One that I will never forget!

Mister briefly became a gentleman and allowed me to place our daughter back into her bassinet. As soon as I drew my hands from her body, I felt Mister's hand tightly wrapping around my hair. I dare not pull from him because it would make him angrier and there was a strong chance that my hair would detach from my scalp. So, I fearfully submitted. As Mister continued to pull my hair, my body began to bend backward.

Mister had gotten on one knee. It was not to propose but to attempt to break my back. He forced my legs to the front side of his knee while my head and arms dangled on the other side. I had now become a contortionist. The more he yelled at me for trying to leave him, the more he stretched me. No matter how many tears ran down my face, I would not get any sympathy from Mister. He then quickly stood up and kept a tight grip on my hair. All I could say to myself was, *Lord, please don't let my baby experience any of this pain. Please let her rest in peace and never learn of this embarrassing moment.*

When I thought it was over, I felt a stiff piece of metal touch my face. It was a gun being placed on my temple. Yep, the fear caught my attention!! I just wanted to be treated like a decent human being. Was that too much to ask? What did he see in me that made him hate me so much? Did I remind him of someone? Did he see my potential and wanted to kill it before it could manifest? Was I an eminent threat? Or was it because he thought he could get away with it? Either way, I survived that night!

I continued going to church, directing the choirs, singing on the radio on Sundays, producing plays, teaching praise dancing, occasionally ministering the word from the pulpit, and placing a mask upon my face to hide my real life.

Once our daughter turned seven months old, my mother-in-law and father-in-law invited Mister and me to take a trip down south with them to visit her sister. Maybe she thought that I could use the break, or it could have been the joy of being around her granddaughter.

I must admit, I was excited. I thought this would be a breath of fresh air for me and maybe this is what Mister also needed.

It was a pleasant ride as we drove south in separate cars. I was glad to have slept and the baby stayed asleep for a while.

We finally made it to our destination, and we could see his aunts, uncles, cousins, etc. I was having a wonderful time. Everything was running so smoothly, and everyone was smiling and laughing. They were reminiscing and just simply loving each other. Yep, this was exactly what I needed to get my husband back on the right track.

We stayed at my husband's aunt's house. We were given a separate bedroom, considering we were married and had a whole family.

We stayed for a few days before it would be time to head back up to New York. On the very last night of our stay, my husband desired to lie down, and I did not feel comfortable for multiple reasons.

One, our daughter would be in bed with us, and two, it was not our bed. I felt that it would be inappropriate, and I expressed it. He did not take it well. I found myself lying in bed with a pillow covering my face. I jumped up and began to fight back, only to lose the battle.

The next morning, it was time to go back to New York, and I was quiet, hurt, and angry. My heart felt like it was literally aching, as sharp pains would pass through. I tried my best to put back on the mask to shield my true struggles.

I tried hard to put a smile on my face, knowing that as soon as we got in the car, tears would run down my face.

I said my goodbyes and climbed into the backseat with my daughter. I hated him so much and desired terrible things to happen to him so that we would never have to experience him or see him in life again.

We pulled away from his family's home and followed his parents back to New York. I noticed that he started falling asleep at the wheel and thankfully my mother-in-law could see it too from her rearview mirror in the other car. She called him on his cell phone and advised him to pull over soon so that he may get into the car with his father and sleep, and in turn, she would drive his car with me and the baby in the backseat.

He pulled over into a safe place and switched cars. As my mother-in-law started driving, I sat quietly. I was so tired and drained from the night before. I forced myself to stay awake to make sure my baby was okay.

Eventually, my mother-in-law began speaking to me and I'm sure it was not a bad conversation. However, I could no longer hold back the tears. I became so overwhelmed. My heart was beating faster and faster. Now and again, it would skip a beat. I felt as if someone wrapped a cord around my neck and pulled it to crush my windpipes. Between the heart palpitations and the panic attack, I finally said the words, "Your son hits me." I did not know how she was going to respond. I stayed frozen as the tears soaked the collar of my dress. I slowly lifted my head and locked eyes with her in the rearview mirror. She looked to be in disbelief and requested that I repeat myself. So, I did. "YOUR son hits me."

I asked her, "Did you hear the banging on the walls?"

She answered with surprise, "No." I continued to tell her about the abuse from the night before and even the abuse I had suffered thus far. The more I spoke, the angrier and more disappointed she became at him.

She then told me that she was going to get him. I became so afraid. Now, I've messed up. I told his mother. What will be the consequences for this one? I quickly had to help her understand that if she says something, he will know that I told her and only God knows what my penalty would be.

My mother-in-law was very smart and most likely worked out in her mind how to approach the issue at hand. We finally arrived back in New York, and it was time to switch back into the car with my husband. However, before that happened, my mother-in-law started fussing at her son. She stated that she knew what he did to me because she was able to hear through the walls and she told him that if he ever put his hands on me again, she would handle him herself. That was a quiet ride home that day!

Chapter 17

A Better Me

As time passed, I started to see less and less of LaSean. He rarely returned my phone calls. Something was wrong and I couldn't put my finger on it. We were like Bonnie and Clyde, Batman and Robin, Cookies and Milk. We were practically joined at the hips, but my guts were telling me that LaSean was not telling me everything.

A Saturday evening came, and it was time for bed. I had a dream about LaSean. I saw him in a classroom setting and no matter how close I tried to get to him, I could not reach far enough. He looked as if he was saying "goodbye." But I paid no mind.

On that Sunday, my husband and I went to church. As we sat in service, our daughter became a bit fussy so, I decided to take her into the church dining room to feed her. As I sat in the dining area, I received news that I could never prepare for. I was told that LaSean had died that morning. I soon reflected on the dream I had earlier and realized that LaSean was really telling me goodbye.

Why did he leave me like that? I never felt pain like that before. I tried to continue feeding my daughter, and I sat in disbelief. I refused to accept what was being said. God, please let me see him one more time. Let me hug him one more time. Please God. God, this is not fair. You said that you would never give me more than I could bear. My heart cannot handle this right now. I won't be able to survive this. I'm just not going to pay attention!

It was now time to go to LaSean's funeral and so many friends, family, and people from the community whose lives he touched showed up. The church was packed and here I was, sitting in the front. By this time, I had known LaSean for approximately seven years and he was my best friend. At his funeral, I refused to open my eyes. Someone came to me and took me by the hand. They walked with me to the front of his casket. I still refused to open my eyes. Then they brought me back to my seat, and I sat back down. Suddenly, I felt my world crumbling. I slowly began to let out a cry. As I clenched my chest, I laid across the bench and curled up into a fetal position. Nothing would soothe my pain.

Afterward, some of us went out to eat and I could not get myself together. It was so bad that my daughter's godmother fed me lies just to help me get through the day. I was so hurt; I took it because I needed it. I didn't care if it wasn't the complete truth. I needed to hold on to possibilities.

My daughter was now two years old, and I hated depending on Mister. I felt I was lacking so much, and it also became quite embarrassing for me to still rely on my mother financially. After speaking with my daughter's godmother, she encouraged me to get a job.

Initially, I tried to get hired at her job which was at Verizon, but I failed the test. She continued to encourage me and eventually, I obtained a receptionist position at Jay H. Tannenbaum, Esq., located on Wall Street in New York City.

In case you didn't catch this early on, currently, I was twenty-three years old, and I did not graduate from high school, so there wasn't a diploma to present to anyone.

When Jay hired me, he knew I did not complete high school, but God allowed him to look past my faults and see my potential. He told me immediately that I would be his receptionist and what that entailed.

Jay taught me how to speak properly and how to think outside the box. He also taught me how to be professional and business minded. There were many times that he would fuss at me for not speaking proper English or when I didn't place enough effort into the task, he had given me. I've shed some tears, but it gave me the strength to stand and learn to do better.

He helped me to understand, not to settle. He surrounded himself with four highly intelligent women. I admired them because they mastered their craft, only to find out they once started out like me. After a while, I started seeking help at an adult center to help me become a better me.

One day, I sang for an event at the adult center and met a gentleman that was able to see my potential. His name was Marvin. I told him I had never finished high school, but I wasn't worried because I had a great job on Wall Street. He smiled and broke down the importance of being independent and doing it for me and my future. He further advised that he was going to do everything in his power to see that I got my high school diploma.

So, between him and his supervisor, they set up for me to attend night school since I was now twenty-four years old going on twenty-five. They could not officially enroll me into night school with high school students. However, the school allowed me to sit in the back of the class and learn by listening but not to participate.

I had passed all my classes and needed to pass one test to obtain my diploma. My daughter was already in a wonderful home daycare that was owned by a pastor's wife. Her name was Mrs. Miller, and she taught my daughter so much, starting from the age of 2 years old. I never had to worry about my daughter because she was in the best hands ever.

I arrived at night school only to be stared at by a bunch of teenagers, but I had a made-up mind that I was going to pass this one test by any means necessary. I left work on Wall Street wearing the best clothes and a fur coat. My hair would stay done, and I would travel with so much finesse and confidence.

CIRCLES

I didn't care about how things looked or how people looked at me. I was going to do this. I took the test twice and failed. I began to become discouraged. I started to think maybe it was just not for me. But giving up was not an option.

My daughter was now four years old, and even though life with my husband wasn't great, I wanted to give my daughter a brother or sister to play with. I became pregnant, and she and her sibling would be five years apart. I was still working for Jay H. Tannenbaum, Esq., when I received the news. I was so excited to be able to produce and it was so awesome to tell my daughter that she was now going to have a sibling.

Even though it was the beginning of my pregnancy, it was quite rough. I was no longer able to work. I stayed nauseous and tired. My mother advised that it would be better to let my daughter stay with her during the week so that she could take her to school, and I would be able to relax a bit more. So, I agreed.

I remember lying on my couch early in the morning sleeping and bringing up all my insides when I received a call from my brother advising me to turn on the television. I then witnessed the second plane going through the world trade center, where I had worked at one time. I just sat on my couch in disbelief. This was close to an event that shall never be forgotten.

I realized that my mother resided in Manhattan, and my daughter was in school in Manhattan as well. I contacted my mother to ask her to pick up my daughter immediately. I couldn't see myself losing either of them. But my mother refused to live in fear and said she would not pick up my daughter early, nor would she leave work early. I was furious, but I could only pray that my daughter and mom would remain safe. I thank God because my little brother was down there when this tragedy occurred, but God spared his life. Not to mention Wall Street wasn't too far off, so God spared my life again.

Chapter 18

You Don't Even Know

I was three months pregnant, and my husband and I were coming from an outing with some friends. By this time, we had now moved once again into another apartment in the Bronx. This time, we had two bedrooms. He became upset because of the attention that I was receiving.

Our friends would not be so blunt to state the actual issue at hand but would make it obvious that I was talented, beautiful, and deserved better. There was one friend, but I see him as my brother, named Mike, and he loved to get a rise out of my husband.

Mike asks me a question like, "What type of man would I consider being a perfect man?" He then followed with another question, but weirdly, he answered it as well. "Would the man have a bald head, long hair, braids, slim built, fat, or muscular? Would he be a singer or a musician? Oh, I know you would like a tall man with long hair and definitely a musician."

This was completely opposite of the traits found in my husband, and he knew it. He was not advising me to cheat on my husband or to find another man, but he was trying to help me understand my worth and that I had options and I never need to feel as if I am to settle. He wanted me to see the beauty that everyone else saw in me. Unfortunately, I couldn't.

My husband sat debating at the dinner table, smiling, and acting as if he was okay with the conversation. But the reality was it was all building up inside of him. They did not know that he was going to be enraged that night. I knew that trouble would come, but I did not know to what extent. I smiled, and I made the best out of that night because I wanted to enjoy the moment. I wanted to feel like I was normal. I wanted to feel what living felt like and being free.

CIRCLES

As soon as we left the restaurant, got into the car, and drove away, Mister began to yell, fuss, and call me names. He degraded me and aimed to make me feel like I was less than nothing. But I kept my mouth closed because I figured people cannot argue alone. Further, I did not want the anger to escalate to another level. I thought that I could keep the peace that way.

Once we arrived in front of the building, he parked the car and continued to fuss, scream, shout, wave his arms, sweat, turn red and ball his fist. He yelled and fussed all the way home. I no longer wanted to stay in the car and take the abuse. I did not become disrespectful, but I let him know that I was getting out of the car and going upstairs.

My stomach, my baby that I was carrying, the child that I was three months pregnant with have now slammed into the gearshift. He grabbed me by both arms as I sat in the passenger seat and pulled me as hard as possible toward him in the driver's seat. Immediately, blood began to pour out of me. A puddle of blood covered the passenger seat. I began to scream and cry, not because I was in pain, but because I did not want my baby to suffer. I did not want to lose my baby.

I told him the blood would not stop and that we needed to go to the emergency room to ensure the baby was okay. He became scared and tried to say it was my fault. Had I not sat so close to the gearshift, this would not have happened. But I knew that's not how the story actually went. I ate every word that he said and remained quiet. I just wanted my baby to be okay and if I wouldn't tell on him that he was the one to cause this damage, he would be okay with taking me to the hospital to ensure my baby was well.

When we arrived at the hospital, I did not provide the truth. I told the doctor and nurses that I had just started bleeding for no reason. I let them know that I was three months pregnant, and that I cared about nothing else but them saving my baby. They placed me on a bed behind a curtain. The pain was so excruciating, but I cared nothing about myself. I wanted to make sure that my baby was okay.

Please tell me that my baby was going to live. I need to know if my baby was going to survive. Please tell me! I cared about nothing else. When the doctor checked me, I asked, "Will my baby be okay? Will my baby live? Will my baby be able to make it?"

She stated to me, "I don't know. We will just have to play it by ear for right now."

That was one of the scariest moments in my life. Even though I may have been just three months, this was my baby. It was a part of me. This was who I was to protect, love, care, teach, raise, keep, hold, and hug. This was my baby, and no one could tell me differently.

God did bless me, and my baby was okay. They released me from the hospital the next morning and my husband tried to make amends. I just wanted to go home to relax and comfort my baby.

One and a half months later, I learned that we were having a baby boy. I was so grateful to hear that. I figured that was perfect. Now I would have a girl and a boy and there's nothing left out there for me to try to get.

I continued to suffer in silence while pregnant with my son, and I didn't focus on myself, my needs, or my desires. I didn't know who I was or what I wanted to be. I just wanted to be safe and sound for both of my children, which mattered to me.

I learned not to rely on Mister, but in all that I was to accomplish; I had to do it on my own. I had to become independent. I began to operate as a mother and father. When I became six and a half months pregnant, my husband, my daughter, and I went to Macy's. I placed my daughter into a cart just in case her legs would become too tired to walk or if she fell asleep. My husband stated that he wanted to go shopping on the next level up in the store. I told him that I would need to take the elevator. He advised that it wasn't that serious and to just place the cart onto the escalator. I listened. (How many know that God always has a ram in the bush?

And praise goes right there!!) At first, all seemed to be going well, but then I realized that as I tried to pop a willy with the cart so that I may get off the escalator, my daughter and I became stuck.

God allowed some children to play on the escalator, and one of them bumped me so hard that it gave me the leverage needed to pick up the cart with my daughter and carry us safely off the escalator. Had that not happened, my daughter would have fallen into the escalator face first.

However, when I lifted the cart, something inside of my body snapped. Something had snapped in the lower part of my abdomen. There was such an unimaginable pain that is still hard for me to describe, but I knew that something was wrong. I went to my husband with tears in my eyes and I said to him, "Something is wrong."

He told me it was in my head and that I was fine. He then advised me to take some Tylenol. I could not ignore the pain. I tried to hold on. I kept pushing my daughter inside the cart, holding on for dear life. When I went to see my doctor, I told her that I heard a clicking sound when I walked. I further advised her that I remained in constant pain.

I told her something snapped inside me and that I wasn't quite sure what it was, but something was wrong. She smiled at me and said, "I have three children of my own and I've never heard of anything like this." So, again, she was one to believe that it was all in my head. That Tuesday, they admitted me to the hospital. A sonogram was performed, and the other doctors realized that my pelvis had separated at six and a half months pregnant. My doctor was told that it wasn't just in my head and that my pelvic bone had separated. I was later told that I would not be able to have a normal delivery, but I would need to have a C-section.

I stayed in pain every day, and separating my legs was exceedingly difficult. I was constantly being monitored because they did not want his head to get stuck and for the pelvic bone to clamp onto his neck, which in turn would stop his breathing. As time passed, they gave me a walker and placed me on bed rest. The bed rest was more painful because now that I moved less, my bones stiffened, making it almost impossible to function. In staying still or laying down, I was not able to move because my bones had locked on me. I had to sit up to sleep.

I was no longer allowed to stay home by myself when my husband went to work. I had to go and stay with my mother so that she, my brothers, and my little sister would help me to function. I was unable to get in and out of cars by myself. There have been times when the pain was so excruciating that I yelled for my brother to come and help me. He slowly sat me up and closed my legs so that I would have less pain. For me to take a bath, I had to take the pillow off my bed and place it in the tub so that I may sit on top of it. However, before I was able to sit comfortably on the pillow, my pelvic bone would hit the pillow before the rest of me would.

Shortly afterward, I was admitted back into the hospital so that they may monitor my baby and me. The pain was so bad; they gave me Percocet to help relieve the pain. I asked the nurse if it was safe for me to take the narcotic while pregnant and she answered, "Yes."

Approximately two or three days had passed, and I had not felt my son move. I was used to feeling him move frequently and I could not understand what was wrong.

I then asked another nurse, "Why don't I feel my baby?" She responded, "It's because you are taking Percocet. It's going directly to him and, more likely, he's at a standstill."

Immediately, I stopped caring about my pain and thought about my child. I refused to take another Percocet or any painkiller as long as my child was in my body. I was not going to suffer and go through all of this and risk losing my baby.

On March 4th, 2002, I went to the hospital to get some blood work done to make sure that I would be ready for my C-section. That evening my water started to leak, and I figured I didn't need to advise anyone because I was going to have a C-section the next day. I was scheduled to give birth on March 5th.

Early in the morning, before the sun would rise on March 5, 2002, I went into full-blown labor. When I finally arrived at the hospital, I was eight and a half centimeters dilated. My doctor was not there yet, so I had to advise another doctor that I was unable to push my baby out due to the circumstances. He then told me that he believed that I could. We argued back and forth and, of course, my husband took his side. I yelled at both and reminded them that I was the one having this baby.

The doctor sent an anesthesiologist so that they may prepare me to have my son. My spine was tapped numerous times, then they laid me on my back for my son to be delivered. By that time, I was able to see a face I so hoped would be there to deliver my son. It was my doctor. As she proceeded to cut my son out of my belly, I laid still in prayer, believing all was going to work out and that my son was going to be born healthy. I was eventually able to see him, and the tears just ran down my face. He made it, thank you God.

The nurses took my son to clean him up as I was being sewn together. Thank you God, all is well. After the recovery room, I was able to go into a regular room. On day one as I lay in my bed, I began to get a little headache and I thought nothing of it but believed this too shall pass. My son is well. On day two, I still had a headache and now the light had become my enemy. This too shall pass. My son is here. On day three, I could no longer lift my head.

I alerted the nurse that this was now happening and that I could not shake it. The nurse expressed the same to my doctor. The doctor came into my room and asked me a couple of questions. He then removed my pillow from my head and laid me straightway onto the bed. He closed the curtains that would shine the light all so bright.

He advised me that he would need to send the anesthesiologist to do a procedure on me. I didn't quite understand what was going on. All I knew was that I was told one percent of women pelvic separates before having a baby, and now one percent of women end up having a spinal headache. I thought to myself, well Lord, I don't know why I must keep being that one percent woman!

Two anesthesiologists came into my hospital room and asked me more questions. They then sat me up in the bed while one stood behind me and one in front.

The anesthesiologist in the front drew blood from my arm and passed the tube of blood to the anesthesiologist in the back of me. That anesthesiologist connected the tube to a line with a needle. They explained that they would need to insert my blood into my spine to clog up holes because the fluid was now leaking down the inside of my back from my brain. They instructed me to sit still, which would be very painful, but I would come through.

The anesthesiologist in front held my hands and tried to converse with me to take my attention away from all I was suffering with at that moment while the other anesthesiologist inserted the needle into my spine. I know what pain is!!

As I felt him inserting the blood into my spine, my legs became heavier and heavier. I told the anesthesiologist in front of me that I could no longer feel my legs but that they felt like bricks.

The anesthesiologist in the front stated to the other anesthesiologist, "Stop what you are doing! This is not supposed to happen." I became paralyzed from the waist down.

The anesthesiologists then advised that they had an emergency C-section upstairs and they would need to come back to me. They laid me down on my bed and placed a sheet on me.

Yes, I was left paralyzed until they returned some hours later. When they came back, they proceeded to perform the same procedure as before, but now this time I became paralyzed from the neck down. They laid me down once again and advised me I would have to remain like that for a while so that the blood may clot the holes in my spine.

Shortly afterward, my mother-in-law came to visit me. I was so grateful to her because she thought it not robbery to feed me and comfort me. I remember hearing her tell her son to go downstairs and get me some flowers for all I'd gone through. He did not.

I appreciate her for how she stood by my side in one of the most challenging times in my life. The doctor told me that my blood level was too low and that I would need a blood transfusion. I refused to receive a blood transfusion, and I told the doctors and the nurses that God was going to move on my behalf. God had brought me through so much in my life that there was no way I was going to doubt him and the power of the Holy Ghost.

The nurse attempted to draw blood out of my arm, but nothing. She also tried my feet, and nothing would come out. She then stated that she would need to go into the veins in my neck to retrieve the blood. My response was, "The devil is a liar." I told her to give me overnight and watch my God bring my blood level to where it needed to be.

My husband and I prayed, read scriptures, and sang songs to God that night. We cried out, believing that God was going to move, and I could not afford to doubt.

The next day, the nurse came in to take my blood and I remained prayerful in my spirit. When she returned, she advised that it went from a five to about a seven, which was abnormal. She was surprised and said, "I don't know what you have been doing but it's working."

I was still paralyzed. I had a catheter inside me for about a week now and it needed to come out before my insides would become damaged. A nurse came and removed the catheter. However, it stayed inside me for so long that I could not urinate. Can you imagine feeling a sensation to urinate and yet it would not release? This was very scary. But I did recognize that God was still in the midst. See, this nurse that removed the catheter was not on duty. She just so happened to be walking past my room and noticed that I had not been eating. The trays of food were just adding up, and no one asked why.

I advised her that I was paralyzed and unable to feed myself. She removed the catheter and sat me on a bedpan. I was able to feel the sensation below, but nothing above. She pulled up her chair to my bedside and pulled the table with the most recent food on it.

As I tell this part of my life, it tears my eyes yet comforts my soul. Tears because of the agape love that she showed me. She was simply an angel and if you were to ask me to describe her today, I couldn't. She patiently fed me while encouraging me that God was going to heal my body and deliver me from this hard time. I told her I was trying to urinate, but it wouldn't come out. She gently spoke to me and said, "Don't worry, it's going to come."

I sat there eating and crying, with a thankfulness in my spirit because I knew that God was smiling on me. After approximately an hour, I began to use the bathroom. The catheter stayed in so long that it almost damaged me for life. But God!!

Finally, I was released from the hospital and can now go home. I was a bit nervous about that because I didn't know what I had to look forward to. My husband picked me and our son up from the hospital and placed him in the car and his car seat. You should know by now that I would not allow my son to sit in the back by himself, so I sat in the back with him. I wanted to make sure that I protected him at all costs.

We arrived at the front of the building and this one move allowed me to understand how things were going to go. Instead of my husband carrying our son upstairs in his car seat, he watched me climb five flights of stairs. Not only did I carry our son in the car seat, but I carried his diaper bag as well. Remember, I had a C-section, so I was still sewn fresh. But God still gave me the strength to survive. When I made it into the apartment, I sat down on the couch in the living room and cried. I found myself in a dark space. I should have been excited to bring home my new baby, but I grew deeper and deeper into depression.

As time passed, I continued to go through my many ups and downs. I had some good days, as anyone else would. But when those bad days came, the good days weren't worth remembering. Please understand that I wasn't totally innocent in all that was going on, but I do believe that a lot of my anger and hatred stemmed from the mistreatment, and I became fed up.

In a sense, I became withdrawn. I was physically around people, but I really wasn't there. I put myself aside because life was no longer for me to live but for my children.

I tried to focus back on my marriage and tried at times to make it work. But the disgust was real. However, through it all, there would soon be something to excite me. My son turned three months, and I received a call that would change my life. "Tammy, you passed your test, and you may now go to your high school and pick up your diploma." I wasn't stupid. I had potential. I was now equal to the other smart people my age. These were the many thoughts that passed through my mind.

The next day I walked into LaGuardia High School with my five-year-old daughter, my three-month-old son, and Mister. I walked proudly because I deserved it. I cried because of how long it took me to accomplish this goal and I stayed the course. When I received my high school diploma, I was 26.

The excitement was now over, and life, reality, came back to the forefront. One night, I lay in our bed, and he started to pick with me. It was rarely over money because he was the breadwinner, and I was the homemaker. Whatever he provided, we learned to be satisfied. But our disagreements would mainly be about sex. He wanted to have sex, but I couldn't forget the many horrific things he had done to me. So, it would kill everything in me to sleep with him.

I became more and more numb to life. I was not happy as long as my children were good, but I survived. He would see the love and affection I gave to my son, and I could see jealousy in his spirit towards his son. He became overly rough. One night he kicked a toy into the room where my son was playing, and the toy hit my son on the forehead, leaving him with a gash that constantly poured out blood.

I became enraged, and he became scared. I yelled at the top of my lungs, "You are taking me and my son to the hospital NOW!" I scared him because he thought I was going to expose him. But I didn't. I just stated that my son has hurt himself for them to stitch him up.

One night while I was lying in bed talking to God in full transparency, Mister came into the bedroom and sat on my side of the bed. He then took a switchblade out and began to swing it quickly over my face. I closed my eyes and was able to feel the wind from the blade. That was not satisfactory enough for him. He then took the pillow from under my head and placed it over my face. I lay with such calmness and peace.

I do not know if I passed out, but I did have a good night's rest and woke up the next morning feeling revived, refreshed, and renewed. I was truly at peace with God, and I did not show fear, nor did I worry. I felt God granting me victory in this situation, whereas the enemy was so angry that he could not destroy me.

CIRCLES

As time went on, I continued to go to church and praise God, aiming to build a stronger relationship with Him. Sometimes I would smile, and it would be genuine, but other times I would just mask my pain and keep it moving.

If I may step back for a moment, when I was pregnant with my son, I expressed to my doctor that I wanted a tubal ligation after having my son. She disagreed and decided it would be best to provide me with an IUD instead. This IUD was to last for ten years. It did not!

Chapter 19

I Hear You Lord

I found myself looking for that string that connects to the IUD but couldn't locate it. I went to the emergency room and told the doctor that I believed I had lost the IUD. As I am saying those very words, she says, "This IUD here?"

My next question was, "Why is it in your hands and not inside of me?" The doctor then gave me a pregnancy test and said, "Congratulations, you are pregnant!" I was in such disbelief I refused to accept her words.

I responded, "Whoever is pregnant, tell them that I said congratulations." The doctor began to get a little upset, yet she gave me the benefit of the doubt and repeated herself. My response was still the same. She ordered me to have an ultrasound and as she moved the transducer around my belly to capture the images, she asked, "Do you see this?" I answered, "Yes."

She said, "That is your baby."

I said, "Whoever is pregnant, tell them I said congratulations." This may seem funny to you, but it was something serious.

The reason that I could not accept being pregnant again was because I was still being abused and it had been only two years since the trauma, I suffered bearing my first son. I could not see myself bringing another life into this world and having to suffer as well. But it was going to happen.

See, this baby was going to be different. There was a purpose for this baby and even though I could not understand the "why" in the beginning God showed me throughout my pregnancy that he would be a different breed. Even with the way he moved in my belly, I can tell this pregnancy was already different. He brought a calmness to me, yet his movement demanded a certain boldness. There was verbal abuse throughout my pregnancy with this baby, but Mister could not touch me while this baby grew within me. My mother named him after a prophet in the Bible.

I struggled to carry my baby boy and had to walk with a walker as well, but it was not as bad as my pregnancy with my first son. Once I had reached 36 weeks my doctor and I discussed when I wanted to give birth because I would have a C-section and tubal ligation. I chose November 16th.

So, the momentous day came for me to have my final child. I was so excited to meet him. This was a scheduled procedure I did not go into labor or had to suffer any pain afterward.

After my doctor delivered him, I felt wonderful. So wonderful that I operated as if I hadn't given birth. It's called drugs (smile). The nurse came into my room to check on me and the next thing I knew she was screaming at the top of her lungs. This was because the stitches had burst, and I could not feel my insides coming out.

By the time I was released from the hospital I had stitches, staples, tape, and glue. Finally, the doctor burned my stomach back together. When I arrived in front of the building, I was left to carry my son in his car seat with his diaper bag. However, mentally I was much stronger this time around. Six weeks passed, and I laid my son beside me at the head of the bed while my husband lay at the foot. "The doctor said that you can start back having sex once the baby turned 6 weeks," he said. My response was I was not ready to start having sex again. I then turned to my side and began to play with my baby. I reminded him of the C-section, tubal ligation, stitches, tape, glue, staples, and the burning together of my stomach. Sex was the furthest from my mind. Mister became so irate he took his foot and kicked me between my legs. Not once, not twice but three times. So much hatred had built up in him. It did not matter that his newborn son was laying right next to me. It did not matter that I was his wife. It did not matter that I just had a serious procedure done. It did not matter that I was simply a human being. How dare I say NO!

My son began to cry, and I understood the cry meant that he was hungry. I slowly stood up and slid my son to the edge of the bed by his feet. I could then scoop him into my arms and lay him on my bosom. Just as I was getting ready to walk out of the bedroom, Mister turned all the lights off in the house by the main switch breaker box.

It's my pleasure to share this with you! First, let me start by saying My God is Great!! Why are you saying that Tammy?

God allowed me to walk to the kitchen in complete darkness, and I bumped into NOTHING. I held my son in my left arm as I gathered everything needed to feed him. As I continued to cuddle him, I poured the gallon of distilled water into his bottle, added two scoops of baby formula, placed the top on the bottle, and shook it to mix well.

Normally, I would heat the bottle but that wasn't a luxury I could afford now. I slowly walked with my son toward the living room and guess what! God allowed the lights to shine into the living room from outside. I sat down on the couch and began feeding my son.

While feeding him, Mister sat directly across from me. I heard the enemy say, "You will never be anything. This is all to your life. You are not even smart. No one will want you. You make me sick. I should punch you in your face right now. You wonder why I am pissed off. You keep playing with me! You don't know anything. You think you are so smart. Keep playing with me. I'm gonna show you something."

As the enemy spoke, I recognized that I intimidated him. I did not have to speak because I could hear God telling me he had me and to be still. As I continued feeding my son, peace came over me and I began to sing and worship the Lord. My son lay tucked away in my arms, he stared me in the eyes and smiled. That was God shining through him.

I then laid my son down on the couch, and I laid on the outside of the couch. Oddly, I was comfortable.

See, that's how great my God is! Amid troubles and adversities, God can grant you peace. When you could have lost your mind, God stepped in and worked it out for you. When you didn't know which way to go, how your rent would be paid, how you would get to work, how you would feed your children, BUT GOD!!

As I lay on the couch, I could hear God telling me that I didn't have to worry or be afraid because he was and still is my protector. Shortly afterward Mister said you can go back to bed now I won't mess with you anymore tonight. Then I heard God confirm it by saying "Go ahead baby he won't mess with you."

I picked my baby up and walked back to the bedroom. Mister turned back on the lights, but I had already returned to the bedroom by this time. I laid my baby on the bed and got on my knees. I started praying to God and as I prayed, I gathered strength. There was such praise and gratitude to God in my spirit.

The words that I prayed that night was, "Lord, anything that is not of you, don't let it cross this threshold. Lord, anyone who is meant to harm me,

DO NOT ALLOW THEM TO CROSS THIS THRESHOLD." When those words left my mouth, I saw a shadow of a foot lift attempting to cross into my bedroom, but it couldn't. Just as soon as the leg lifted to attempt to place the foot across the threshold was as fast as it took to pull it away.

See there is power in our tongue. That night I learned it firsthand. I spoke life over me and my children and I pleaded the blood of Jesus against Satan and all his demonic forces. I stood bold in what I said, and I refused to back down.

Chapter 20

I Feel My Help Coming On!

After that last incident with Mister, I became empowered. I understood that I was more powerful than I was told. This did not mean that the abuse stopped. However, instead of allowing the rocks to gather over and bury me, I placed each rock under my feet to help elevate me higher. Before I knew it, I was standing on a mountain that the enemy meant for my demise.

Sunday morning came, and it was time to get me and the kids ready for church. Mister drove us all to church. That morning, I simply pissed him off. He couldn't decide if he should wait until we got home to inflict pain or if he would get away with it in front of the church building. Mister was now taking chances for others to see who he was. A man of God? I think not.

As I stepped out of the car and proceeded to walk through the church doors, Mister quickly blocked me. I soon found my torso hemmed up to the iron gates that secured the church building. For the many sisters and brothers that passed by on their way to service, Mister granted the illusion that we were just having a peaceful conversation. I knew differently. The conversation went like this:

Deacon: Good morning, guys!

Mister: Praise the Lord, my brother

Sister: Hey y'all. Do you need me to take the kids inside? (smile)

Mister: No thank you. We will soon be in!

Sister: Okay

Mother in the church: (looks, says nothing, and goes into the church)

The whole time this charade was going on, Mister smiled while he forcefully held my torso against the iron bars. When no one was looking, his whole face and voice changed. He talked out the side of his mouth as spit followed. He whispered continual threats and occasionally shook the gate, which bounced off my back as if we were playing a ping-pong game and my back represented the table.

Finally, I was released by Mister and granted permission to go inside the church. This was the day I desired more than anything to seek help. After service, I went to a "Mother" in the church, and I told her what have been going on. I just believed that she was going to impart wisdom and that everything was going to be alright. However, her response was surprisingly off.

She advised me to keep praying and that things would get better in my marriage. As if it was normal for a man to beat a woman. I was not looking for her to say leave my husband, but I could not understand why she thought this behavior was acceptable. Was this her life, and she learned to live with it? Was she taught that you are to remain with your husband, no matter what he may do to you? Well, this was not acceptable to me!

Our last son had turned two years old and was as bold as he could be. One evening as I stood in the living room, Mister walked towards me as if he would hit me. Our son raised his little hand and stuck it straight out. His voice was small, but his impact was on a greater scale. He then said, "STOP!" Mister stopped dead in his tracks and walked away.

That night really did something to me. I was supposed to protect my baby, and here he was standing up to protect me at age 2. I felt like I had failed him.

December 28, 2006, came, and I already gave my children to my mother for winter recess. I was scheduled to sing at a funeral that night. I was grateful because it was a paid engagement, and I needed the money. After I sang, I went to my children's godmother's home, which was just around the corner, to have some girl time.

We sat down and watched movies, talked, ate, and laughed. This girl's night was very much needed. Her house phone rang. It was Mister calling to confirm that I was at her home. He seemingly didn't have a problem with me being there. She confirmed and further advised that we were having a great time. Mister hung up the phone.

Approximately an hour passed, and her phone rang. It was Mister once again. He asked when I would be coming home, and she said, "soon." She then advised Mister that she would place me in a cab to come home at that moment and that she did. When Mister called back the third time, we both were frustrated.

As I rode in the cab, I felt a bit different that night. I had a smile on my face but sadness in my heart. You may say, Tammy, you've expressed that same feeling before. However, I felt in my gut that something about this night would be different.

As the cab drove closer to my house, I heard instructions to place the money I made that night from the funeral into my bra. I did it! The cab pulled up in front of the building and I stepped out. I went upstairs and unlocked the front door. I walked into the house and investigated each room to see where Mister could be. He was nowhere to be found.

I then picked up the phone and called my children's godmother to tell her that I had made it home safe and to further advise that Mister was not home. We said goodnight and hung up the phone. The next instruction I could hear was for me to place my wallet with my identification in a small Victoria's Secrets bag with a change of clothes, fresh underclothes, and my coat. I was to sit all these items against the wall that was directly facing the front door. I did it!

I then went into my bedroom and put on my nightgown, but I did not take off my bra. I went back into the living room and sat on the couch to prepare for my interview scheduled for the next day. Suddenly, I heard Mister's key turning in the door. Before I could stand up, he pushed the door open with such force and ran towards me. I couldn't understand why he needed to race toward me, but I was afraid for my life.

He then proceeded to kiss me as he aggressively reached under my gown to pull my panties down. The more he attempted to pull down my panties, the more aggressive he became. I could feel him scratching me, causing my thigh to burn, and at the same time, he used his weight to pin me to the couch. I didn't understand what was happening at this time, but I knew that this wasn't love.

I fought with everything in me. Out of everything I had suffered in life thus far; rape would not be one of those things. I was scared for my life, but I could no longer bow down.

Mister angrily stood up as if he saw no wrong in what he was attempting to do. He yelled that it was his right and that I was to submit. I grabbed my already packed bag and started to walk to the door to leave, but he jumped in front of the door and blocked me from leaving. I was then able to see how this night was going to go (or so I thought).

I walked back to the living room and called my children's godmother. She answered, but then he snatched the phone out of my hand and slammed it back on the hook.

I felt bad for calling her this time of the morning, seeing that she had recently given birth. She knew that something was wrong, so she called back, and I answered the phone. "He won't let me out, Teresa," I cried. Mister soon went into a room that he made into his office and picked up the other phone. He began to explain to Teresa why he was so angry and couldn't just let me go.

So, I got back on the phone and apologized. I told her not to worry and that I would be okay. I walked into my bedroom and lay on the bed. I could still hear Mister explaining his behavior. Suddenly, he went from explaining to what he would do to me.

Mister said, "I know what I am going to do. I am going to kill her tonight. I am going to stab her with my machete."

The next instruction I heard was to get out of bed, slowly walk towards the already packed bag, and put on my coat. I did! Mister's office was directly across from the front door, so I had to ensure he didn't know I was standing there.

I gently placed my back against the wall as I held the two straps connected to my Victoria Secrets bag. As I listened to Mister's threats, I could also hear Teresa's plea for my life. She asked him to allow me to stay with her for the night and promised I would return the next day. Mister was not falling for it.

I looked at the locks on the front door and I realized something. Every day and night, Mister ensured all three locks remained locked. However, because he rushed into the house earlier, he forgot to place all the locks on the door. I could see that it was only one active lock on the door. The bottom lock was the easiest lock out of all the locks because all I had to do was turn it.

I slowly peeked into Mister's office to see which way he was facing. Thankfully, he was facing away from the front door. I thought to myself, this was my moment! I couldn't freeze up now. It was now or never! I quietly tiptoed towards the front door while every now and again glancing back to make sure Mister wasn't looking. There was no turning back. Giving up was not an option. The only thing I was sure of in that moment was that I would run because my life depended on it. One more step and I finally made it to the door. As I raised my freed hand to caress the bottom lock, I looked back one more time. Ready, set, click, and go!

No time to take a breath. No time to think. It doesn't matter which way you run, just keep going! Tammy, you are almost there. One more flight, one more flight! Push. You will make it! I got you, baby. I am here! Keep going! God help me! Please don't let him get me. The many thoughts that ran through my mind.

I ran out of the building and Mister caught me by the back of my neck and flew me towards the next building as if I was just an old dirty rag. Mister demanded that I go back upstairs. My thought then was that my mom had my children, and they would be well taken care of. So, if he was to kill me, my babies would remain safe.

I screamed, "No!" Even though I had some fear, I was simply tired of my life. There was a part of me that waited for help from those that were outside, but they never budged, just watched. Here I am at three o'clock in the morning, being made to feel like I was less than human, and no one had enough compassion to say, "stop" or to call the police.

Mister grabbed my hand and proceeded to break my fingers. I was able to gather enough strength to pull my hand away. I then took all my rings off my finger, including my wedding ring, and told Mister that he was no longer my husband, and I was no longer his wife. I gave him the rings, and he snatched my bag from me. I was still afraid, but I had a made-up mind that this was going to be my exit and I would never return. I stood up and began to walk through the South Bronx in my nightgown, flats, and fur coat. I was cold and tried to avoid stepping in large piles of snow, but I was walking toward my freedom, so none mattered.

As I walked back towards Teresa's house, my mind was blank, but somehow my feet kept moving. I didn't have a plan, but I knew that it was God that provided the instructions for me to escape. I told you that this night was going to be different. (smile)

I finally made it to Teresa's building and Mister followed me every step of the way. I made it to Teresa's apartment and knocked on the door. She opened it and I walked in. Just before she could close the door, Mister placed his foot in the door. She then said, "Mister, please move your foot from my door." Mister explained why he was there, but she would not acknowledge anything he had to say at this point. She then said, "Mister, you don't want me to call Big Ty, do you?" Mister's tune changed immediately, and he removed his foot from the door.

I went into Teresa's bedroom and sat on her bed. For hours, I stared at her walls. I cannot remember a single thought that passed through my mind from this time. I remember my eyes were so swollen, I couldn't stop shaking. I was so tired, but I forgot how to close my eyes and sleep. I could feel the tears streaming down my face, but it was useless to wipe it because more would follow.

Teresa's husband finally came in from working through the night. He walked into the bedroom and sat in a rocking chair that faced me. He said, "Cuz, I'm sorry. I didn't know. You will never have to worry again. I got you; you dig?" Something special about when my big cousin said those words to me made me feel free and protected.

I found myself weeping like a baby. I slowly tilted to the side as my body began to melt in their bed. I remembered what sleep was and even though the tears kept falling, I was able to rest awhile.

Chapter 21

Vigilante

Teresa and her husband welcomed me and my three children into their home with open arms. For the first time in ten years, I was able to breathe. I had no idea how life would take me, but I was grateful to be alive and have my children.

A few days passed, and Teresa thought it would be good for me to get some fresh air, so she invited my daughter and I to ride with her to her grandmother's home. When we arrived, I did not want to leave the car. She understood and said that she would be right back.

Night had fallen, and I quietly remained seated. Suddenly, out of my peripheral vision, I could see what seemed to look like a woman's body being tossed over a bench. Before I knew it, I was out of the car and walking towards the bench. Not only was this poor body tossed over a bench, but then I saw the same body being dragged to the ground and punched. My attention briefly left the body and zoomed in on a stroller. This was a young mom being abused and, in that stroller, lay her newborn baby.

I did not stop to think about what could happen to me if I were to intervene. I did not create a plan. I simply remembered, and that gave me all the strength and courage I needed.

Well, this queen would not suffer like I did because I made a vow within myself that I would protect women at all costs. I remembered the moment that everyone stood around and watched Mister make the attempt to destroy me. Yet, no one was bold enough to come to my rescue.

"You may take your baby and go, my sister," I spoke. She looked at me with confusion. "You may go wherever you need to go. I will handle him." I spoke.

"Mind your business!" She spoke. Now, I was the one confused. I thought maybe she didn't understand me or maybe she thought I was crazy. Either way, I was too deep in it now to stop.

I tried one more time to free her from this "monster", but she refused to accept freedom. It was almost as if she thought that she deserved the beating. I realized that to save her and the baby, I would have to address her abuser.

Hey, my brother, why are you beating her? What has she done that was so bad? He looked at me with a cold stare as he held her hair wrapped around his fist.

"Is that your baby in the stroller?"

"Yes," he answered. I soon realized that he was angry at the woman, but still cared about the baby. I needed to appeal to his fatherly side.

"My brother, I do not know what made you angry. But it is really cold out here and just for the sake of your baby, would you allow her to take the baby into a warm place?"

I wasn't sure if this tactic would work, but I had to try. He slowly unraveled her hair from his clutched fist and ordered her to take the baby inside. With her head hanging low, she slowly walked over to the stroller and began to push. In passing, she took a moment to raise her head just to glance into my eyes. I could read her pain, embarrassment, fear, and gratefulness. I pray that she was able to read my unconditional love for her and her baby.

However, the young man wasn't so lucky! I left him in the midst of an angry mob that decided to seek justice their own way. All the while this was going on, I could hear my daughter saying, "No Ma, no!"

Tammy Flowers-Hollis

I couldn't explain what came over me. There was no more fear!! No more just accepting!! It was time for a change.

Chapter 22

Time To Move From Here

I came back home with Teresa and though I was grateful for all she and her husband were doing for my children and me, I felt like I was becoming a burden. They showed so much love and compassion during what may be considered one of the most pivotal parts of my life. But I didn't want to overstay my welcome. I had to step out on faith. But how was I supposed to do that? What would be my next move?

My mother-in-law asked me and my children to come and stay with her for a weekend. I agreed. During that time, she showed me what a true woman and mother was. She did not take the side of her son. Instead, she advised me to do what I needed to do for the safety of myself and my children.

Living with my mother was not an option. It would allow me to become an easy target. I needed to go into hiding because Mister made it clear that he would not give up. I reach out to the Domestic Violence Hotline with nowhere else to turn. I did not know what to say or expect, but I knew that I had to move from this place.

By the grace of God, they accepted my children and me into a domestic violence shelter. The first day I arrived, I didn't know how to feel. So many emotions ran through me. The case manager walked me and my children to where we would be staying for the next year. As we stood in the middle of the floor, I couldn't help but feel a sense of guilt.

I took my children from a three-bedroom apartment, their school, their friends, and all that they knew. For what? Was I being overly dramatic? Did I take this too far? Was it really that bad? Am I being a wonderful mom or am I inflicting unnecessary pain on my children? Am I a bad person for taking them away from their father? Should I have tried to work it out one more time? Will my children hate me because I could possibly be ruining their lives, or will they understand that I was trying to protect them? Will my family be upset with me? How will we survive?

The more I pondered on it, the more the tears soaked my shirt. I turned around and looked at Ms. Thomas, yes that was her name, and began to express my regrets. I felt like an absolute failure. I couldn't stop crying. I was embarrassed and felt so lost.

I soon felt a gentle rub on my arm. Ms. Thomas pulled me closer and laid my head upon her bosom. She spoke these words, "If you go back, he will kill you and then your kids won't have a mother. But if you stay, they will have a mother and father."

She smiled and left the room so that my children and I could get acclimated to our new home. I wiped my eyes and looked at my children. "This will be our new home, guys."

They didn't hate me! On the contrary, they smiled as if they were ready for peace of mind as well.

Chapter 23

It's Not About Me

Prior to going to a shelter, my children and I had never experienced food stamps or welfare. This was because Mister took care of us. I was not embarrassed or cocky but felt out of my element. I went to Social Services to complete an application for food stamps and welfare. The treatment was horrible, I must say. Even though no one there knew what I had gone through, there was simply no compassion. I felt as if they were treating me like a number rather than a human being. There were questions that I didn't know how to answer. Not because I was slow, but because I never had to answer such questions.

I walked over to a woman that worked there and I advised that I didn't understand all that was being asked of me. Her response was, "You should be used to it by now!" Her words pierced my very soul.

I then responded, "Why should I be used to welfare? Why would you speak to me as if I was uneducated, lazy, and looking for a handout? Be careful how you treat people because you never know where you may end up one day and you just might need one of us to help you!" I further advised her that I was a domestic violence victim and that I didn't volunteer for the position. She then apologized and began to treat me like a human being.

In just a few days, I was on welfare, receiving food stamps and they approved my protective order. My children and I went grocery shopping, and they were so excited because they were able to pick out some of their favorite foods and snacks. I continued to smile because it brought joy that my children were happy, but I quickly moved from a size 16 to a size 0.

No matter how much I smiled, I was still broken. I tried not to show my struggle in front of my children, but the bags under my eyes told on me. For a moment, I found myself in a state of, "Woe is me." I didn't complain but wanted to understand the "*why*?"

As we carried the groceries into the shelter, I saw a woman that was missing a breast. As I continued to walk down the hall, the next woman had a thick scar that started from the corner of her eyebrow towards her nose. Her abuser used a sharp tool to cut her eye out. I finally made it to the front of my room and there another woman stood. She was so full of life and accepted what she couldn't change. This would be an enormous gash in her stomach. Her abuser opened her up and left her to die.

Seeing the horrific scars that these women had to live with every day of their lives and being reminded daily of how they were incurred was amazing to me. These weren't just women, but they all were mothers too.

A still small voice spoke to me and said, "Take a look at these women. Do you see their scars? I need you to remind them that I have allowed them to survive. I am here for them, and I love them."

I then heard, "Tammy, this was not a punishment for you. I allowed you to go through all that you have gone through to prepare you for this and more. They would not have listened to you if you hadn't come with the experience. You survived. You are not dead! I have kept you this far and I shall continue. You shall never worry about provision because I shall continue to provide. However, I need you to not think about yourself. Come away from this pity party that you are trying to have. I need you to minister to every woman you encounter. That includes the staff as well. You are here to remind some and introduce others to me."

Almost immediately, women began to line up at my door and I always found a word of encouragement for them. I fed them, prayed with them, cried with them, supported their dreams, and whatever else God allowed me to do. From that day on, I understood that my name was unimportant, but my service was.

I received an invitation to speak with the head of the shelter. Her name was Dr. Grove. I didn't know the reason, but I had to find out. I walked to her office and lightly tapped on the wooden door. I was a bit nervous but didn't believe I'd done anything wrong. She permitted me to open the door and to have a seat.

"Hi Tammy, my name is Dr. Grove, and I have heard many things about you," she said.

I was still nervous because I didn't know what that meant and what to expect. "Tammy, you have been such a blessing and an encouragement. I would like to know if you would be willing to go to some of our other hidden locations and encourage those women as well?"

My heart dropped. This powerful and educated woman just asked little ole me if I would be willing to help other women. This not only meant that she trusted me to empower these women, but she trusted me enough to know that I would never expose the locations or place any of the women in harm's way. I was grateful for this opportunity.

At one of the locations, I wore a nice dress, heels, a fur coat, and my hair nicely braided. I walked into what they considered the community room, and it was full of women. I was a bit nervous because I didn't know if the women would be receptive to what I had to say. Think about it, some women were older than me and possibly knew more than me. But I didn't let that stop me. It wasn't about me, but about the queens that sat before me.

When I first began to speak, some of the women smiled and others looked to have an attitude. Finally, one queen raised her hand and said, "How can you come up inside here trying to give us a pep talk? You don't know anything about this life! Look at you in your fancy clothes. You have the nerve to a fur coat and want to act like you understand us. Go somewhere with that!"

Her words made me smile. It was God's way of opening the door for me to walk right on in. "Thank you so much, my sister, for your compliments. You have allowed me to know that I look good and that I don't look like what I've been through."

I further shared that my dress and shoes cost me $5.00 from a thrift store. The fur coat I wore was the same one I wore when I escaped with my life from my abuser. He bought it when I was married to him. I went to the hair store and purchased three packs of synthetic hair for $3.15. I cut the hair in half to make it stretch and I just finished braiding my hair this morning.

CIRCLES

LESSON 1:

Never judge a book by its cover.

Just because you have gone through some things doesn't mean you must look like it.

You don't have to spend a lot of money to look good.

Never box yourself in (I am a…I became a runway model, hairstylist, motivational speaker, and financial advisor all in one day.) (*smile*)

Now, I had their attention. I shared my experiences with them, and they felt safe to share their experiences with me. We bonded over our tragedies, but I was determined to arise from that place. We did not stay there. Even though we suffered through it, the keyword was "THROUGH." Which meant we had survived. It was now time to figure out our "NEXT." This was a hard topic for all of us because we couldn't see ourselves becoming a butterfly, even though we broke through the cocoon. Some felt like they deserved to experience a great life; sadly, some felt they didn't deserve anything good. Some women believed that they brought it on themselves and that had they operated differently, their abuser would have treated them better.

I tell you; we were an absolute mess. BUT we pressed our way and found peace. We created realistic goals. No goal was too small. One goal was to step outside and allow the sunlight to hit her face. Another goal was to look into a mirror.

These may seem a bit simple but to one who has suffered and has not been able to accomplish these goals because of fear or feeling ugly, IT'S HUGE!

LESSON 2:

Sometimes we take advantage of things by counting them as small without understanding that it's not small to someone else.

Whether you take a small step or a giant leap, it counts.

That day, I felt like I served my purpose. The more I shared, the more I became aware of the process that God was allowing me to go through. I was able to see God's hand. This did not mean I was healed or no longer cried. On the contrary, I continued to cry and sometimes suffered through depression and anxiety because this journey was not easy.

LESSON 3:

Sometimes, amid our brokenness, we tend to be stronger for others than ourselves.

When you speak your truth, you have now entered your healing process.

Tears are not a sign of weakness. There is strength in your tears.

God did not allow you to survive and not have a purpose.

They invited me to speak at a Domestic Violence Awareness Seminar located at the infamous John Jay College of Criminal Justice in New York City. I was presented with an award and interviewed by a news reporter. There wasn't a dry eye left in the room. I didn't want to leave the building without acknowledging that I was there because of the grace and mercy of God. So, instead of continuing to speak, I began to sing, "To God Be The Glory."

I cannot take credit for anything. It's not because I'm smart or a good person. God spared me, even though I didn't deserve it.

God continued to bless me as I continued to speak and share what he has given me. I received a few more awards throughout my stay with the shelter.

Chapter 24

You're A Boss

I enrolled my two oldest children in school and my baby in daycare. This left time for me to obtain a job. They hired me to work at a nonprofit organization to assist with job placement for those that lived in a shelter. The irony was that I lived in a shelter as well, but they did not know it. So, I was helping men and women work towards having a better life, but every night I had a curfew just like them.

My mother played (and still plays) a huge role in my children's upbringing. I took all my children to my mother in the early mornings. She fed them breakfast and took them to school. Once school was over, she picked all of them up from school, fed them dinner, helped with their homework, bathed them, and entertained them until I picked them up.

The job that I had paid well, but I needed more. They hired me for a second job as an After-School Assistant Teacher to tutor kindergarteners and first-grade students. That was about 9-12 hours a week, but the hourly rate was higher than my first job. With the combination of both jobs, I was no longer eligible for welfare, and I was okay with that.

As time passed, I was hired at a small church in Harlem to teach the children, adults, and sometimes a combined choir. It brought me so much joy. While teaching those choirs, another church also hired me to teach them. Before I knew it, I was teaching 12 different choirs. I never became confused about the songs I taught, or the choir scheduled.

God is so amazing! Some people would call it "church hopping" or being in it for the money, but God's plan was much more than man could fathom. God allowed me the opportunity to learn more about him firsthand. There was no one specific pastor or church to attach myself to. I had to seek God for myself and his teachings. God was pulling me away from traditions that were created by man but not located in His word.

Many times, in growing up, we learn from either our parents, pastors, church folks, etc., and we take them at their word because we assume they know better or more. But God was starting to show me that age was just a number and that I was meant to be bold and stand for HIS truth. I had already experienced God by this time, but to experience being bold enough to stand for God and sometimes just looking plain ole crazy made it all worth it.

I was free to worship without an explanation. I was able to see the hands of God clearly. Best of all, God blessed me to understand that it was imperative that I didn't support the division in the churches, but to know that there is one body of CHRIST with many members. It was not important for me to have a title or to be acknowledged. I am obligated to do my part as being a part of the body of CHRIST.

Chapter 25

I Have Power!!

O ne day I ran into my god-sister, whom I hadn't seen in about a year. I shared with her that my children and I were living in a shelter and why. She held me tightly in her arms. It pained her to know that was my life. She had now resided in Pennsylvania. She then invited me to come to Pennsylvania. Of course, we knew at that time it was impossible because I was obligated to follow the shelter's rules. But we stayed in touch.

Going back to the shelter broke my heart even more. What's wrong with me? Can I not do anything right? Is this all to my life? How long will I be stuck in this position? I'm a grown woman living under a child's rule. I can't go as I please. Is this really good for me?

See, even though life may seem to be going well, sometimes you can still have those moments of going backward. Again, it's a process. I did not forget the goodness of Jesus, but I did have those moments of wondering if all of this was worth it. I don't want to come across as if everything was just peachy.

I found myself continuously going back and forth to court with Mister. I was doing well until I knew I would see his face and my body would just give out. One day we were scheduled for court, and I went to the courthouse, stepped into the elevator, stepped out of the elevator, and no longer could I catch my breath. The air became so thick it had a chokehold on me.

The courthouse lights became dim as I slid down the wall next to the elevator. No matter how much I separated the neck of my blouse from my throat, I could not grasp the air. After the security guard and other good Samaritans sat me on a chair and helped me relax, I learned I had suffered a panic attack. This was simply me realizing that I would see Mister that day.

Oh, I forgot to tell you something! The president of the nonprofit organization I worked for promised me and my children a three-bedroom apartment. The organization owned properties, and the president advised that he would be able to accept my voucher and allow him to have the apartment renovated so that it would be acceptable to live in. (Keep that in mind)

A little over a year had passed, and the shelter could not place me into tier 2. So, I was now placed in another shelter, but it was not a domestic violence shelter. It was a family shelter. This meant that there were men incorporated into this shelter as well.

The first day I entered and went to sign myself in, I was advised that I was in the wrong place by the security guard. I then asked why he felt that I was not supposed to be there. He responded, "We don't get people that look like you." I was a bit baffled, but I understood what he was trying to say. He was implying that I was too clean and put together to belong in such a place as a shelter. I then advised him that I was where I was supposed to be.

More time had passed, and the courts awarded Mister weekend visits. I took the children to my mother's home, and he would pick them up from there. The shelter honored the court order and permitted me to stay out for the weekend as well. I was now able to travel to Pennsylvania.

Every chance I had; I found a way to land in Pennsylvania. My godmother was the Pastor and Founder of Liberty Worship Center, which was in Allentown, PA. It was a breath of fresh air and a life I had never experienced before. She was bold with her words and carried a lot of wisdom, beauty, and compassion. She did not allow self-pity, but she encouraged honesty and strength. My god-sister was and is still my big sister. These two women together were a powerhouse. They taught me how to love myself and how to become a stronger woman.

CIRCLES

There were so many tears I shed, and at times, I couldn't see how I was going to make it as a woman or a mother. However, they would not allow me to give up. One weekend, I took my sons to Pennsylvania and my god-sister drove us to an apartment complex. She then walked me into the property manager's office and introduced me to her. She soon asked if I would like to see their available apartments. Without hesitation, I said, "Yes!" I was not considering moving because I had an apartment waiting in New York.

She handed me the keys, and I was surprised because she did not know me but because she knew my god sister, that was good enough. My sons and I walked over to what they considered a complex. However, where I was from, this was considered a house. I placed the key in the lock and opened the door. This place was enormous. I was overjoyed when I watched my sons roll around on the carpeted living room floor. They were so happy and were free to be children. However, I started to become a bit weary because I could see their joy, but this was not our home. I did not know the first thing about renting an apartment.

I told my god-sister that I felt dumb because I felt I should have known more than what I knew. I never paid a bill until I moved into the shelter and had my first cellphone bill. Other than that, I started to believe what Mister had said that night. "You will never be anything. This is all to your life. You are not even smart."

My god-sister held me in her arms and rebuked every negative word that was spoken over me. She then expressed that God sent me there so that she and my godmother would be able to help me. She assured me that even though I may have felt lost then, it would not always be like that.

She suggested that I apply for the apartment in Pennsylvania. The property manager advised that the application and background check would cost a total of $100. We went to the bank and lo-and-behold, there was exactly $100 in my bank account. We went back with a completed application and the $100. I was going to drop it off, but the property manager said she could do the background check while I remain in the office. So, I did.

As I sat in the waiting room and looked towards the wall, my credit was being checked behind me in a small office. I didn't know what a background or credit check meant. I didn't get excited because I just knew she would come back to me with a rejection. However, as the stapler clicked down, I heard the words, "It's yours!" The property manager walked from her office behind me and came around towards the front of me as she handed me the papers and said, "It's yours!" I began to cry uncontrollably, and I asked her if it would be okay to give her a hug. She answered, "Yes."

She was unaware of all I had suffered through at that time and I'm sure I seemed a bit crazy, but this was a great time during my journey.

I returned to New York and signed back into the shelter. I continued living in the shelter and was still viewing apartments that were scheduled by the shelter. Between spending time with my family and friends in Pennsylvania and attending church, life was starting to really look up.

I started receiving weird texts. I did not know who was on the other end, but it was obvious that they were not happy with me. I received a lot of texts regarding hurting Teresa. Whoever this was, understood that she had my heart and to hurt her meant you were hurting me. Why would this person do these things? I could not understand.

One evening, I received a text threatening to kill Teresa. Whoever this was, it was clear that they knew who she was. The text further advised that I should give her a call because she was home alone. I immediately called her, and she was just fine. Then the text read to tell her to answer the intercom. While we were on the phone, someone suddenly rang the intercom downstairs. I yelled, "Don't answer!" This was very traumatizing for both of us. I felt like we were in a horror movie, and someone was destined to be hurt. Another instance was when this person advised that Teresa was going to be taken care of. I called her again, and she said some one tried to run her off the road.

This was becoming more serious, and I couldn't understand why this was happening. This person seemed to know her every move, and they kept me posted on every attack. Her intercom was pressed almost every night, so that allowed me to know that this person also knew her husband's work schedule.

This attack went on for a couple of months. I refused to be defeated by an enemy that was a flat-out coward. I prayed and asked the Lord to show me who this was, and I stood still and waited for the answer.

One evening I walked into the shelter and heard as clear as day, "Tammy, it's him." I continued walking towards the front desk to sign in and heard it again. "Tammy, it's him."

As I began to sign my name, I looked up at the security guard and said, "I know that it's you."

He looked at me puzzled and said, "What are you talking about?"

I then replied, "I know!" I stayed still as I looked him in his eyes.

He then said, "How did you know it was me?"

I told him because the Lord told me so and I walked away. I refused to give any of my power away.

The next day was a Tuesday. I received another text, and it now read, "So, just because you know it's me doesn't mean that I am going to stop. Your sister will die today!"

Teresa didn't answer the phone when I went to call her. I called numerous times but got no answer. I received another text advising me that she will never answer a phone again. All the while, I was standing in front of the church, waiting for rehearsal to start.

I became enraged. I made a special phone call that would take this guy out of here. Just when I hung up my phone, Teresa pulled up in her truck. I was happy and angry at the same time. I practically jumped through her car window and cried, "Why didn't you answer your phone? Do you know how scared I was? I thought that you were dead!" Then I saw scratches on her neck. "What happened? I'm glad I did what I did."

Teresa asked, "What did you do Sis?"

I replied, "I took care of it. You will never go through anything like this again. No one will bother you going forward."

She then told me to cancel my plans, and that she was okay. She advised that the guy had his wife or girlfriend come to her job to fight her. He lied and made it as if Teresa liked him and she wouldn't leave him alone.

Thankfully, she was able to express the truth to the young lady and instead of the lady being upset with her; she realized that it was the man who actually lied.

Teresa convinced me to not go through with my plans and I called it off. It took everything to humble myself and allow God to fight this battle for me. I still couldn't understand why this man that worked in the shelter as a protector hated me. How did he get my number? How did he know where Teresa lived? How did he know where her job was? How did he know when her husband was not at home? Yet, I did not know him.

As time passed, Mister and I were still going to court. This particular day, Mister decided to share some information with the judge, and one thing stayed with me. He said, "Your honor, I have a friend who works in the shelter she stays in." This statement answered all my questions pertaining to who and why I was put through this. I did not cry, but it allowed me to see that I was a threat. I refused to give away my power!

I continued to go back and forth to Pennsylvania on the weekends and the more I went, the more I fell in love and found peace. Each trip strengthened and encouraged me. I continued working for the nonprofit organization, the after-school teacher and choir directress, and I provided vocal coaching for individuals as well. I was able to maintain these positions for 2 years.

While living in the shelter, the room where my children and I stayed was infested with bedbugs. Before entering this shelter, I'd only heard of bedbugs in a song but never knew they existed. The bedbugs were so huge it was obvious that they had been living inside the wood within that room for a very long time. These bugs violated my children and me every night and I had to find a solution to eliminate them.

I've heard of how dangerous it was to combine bleach and ammonia. That it forms a gas. I was so desperate I was willing to try anything. I combined the two into a plastic spray bottle. I placed all three of my children in the bed with me and as they slept, I remained awake to watch over them and make sure they did not get bitten. I constantly cleaned and sprayed down the bed in hopes that the infestation would cease. It didn't.

One day I went to work and saw a bedbug crawling on my shirt as I stood in the bathroom. I left out crying, feeling disgusted and embarrassed. I became so stressed out I could no longer keep myself together to stay at my job.

There was just so much that was going on in my life at one time, it was hard to stay focused. I felt myself being pulled every which way but loose. Before I knew it, I had a nervous breakdown.

Chapter 26

Come Home

I realized that in all that I was doing, I never took the time out to address my issues. It was easier for me to help others, to focus on other people's problems, to sing and direct choirs, and to teach children rather than to face my own issues. I figured I wouldn't have to deal with my issues if I kept moving around and doing things (you know, staying busy). What I was doing was running away.

I realized the moment that I would stand still long enough, it would force me to remember my real life and my actual struggles. I did not want to look at myself in the mirror because it would force me to see the truth. The truth was not something I wanted. I wanted to move on from then on and start my life over. I did not want to be reminded of watching my father hurt people and sometimes they couldn't recover from the damage he had inflicted. I did not want to be reminded of being molested by multiple people that I still had to be around. I did not want to be reminded of how much of a whore I have been. I did not want to be reminded of placing men before my children.

This is when generational curses became obvious to me. They passed this baggage and more down to me and now I was passing it down to my children. It was like looking at a bunch of dirty t-shirts on the ground and I would pick up a t-shirt and put it on (each t-shirt represented trials I've suffered through) I would then pick up another t-shirt and place it on my daughter and then she would pick up a t-shirt and place it upon her daughter. Before you know it, I would have on T-shirts as well as my daughter and now my granddaughter. No one addressing the core issues but mastering the coverup. It just felt easier that way. However, it took a certain boldness to remove pride and to understand I needed to be honest because I needed help. I was close to losing my mind. I tried to do it all on my own, but the more I tried, the more overwhelmed I became.

CIRCLES

I could not continue to stay in the shelter and suffer alone. My mother welcomed me and my children with open arms after I called her. I was relieved to be around my mother more. I needed her strength. This also allowed me to travel back and forth to Pennsylvania much more.

I worshipped with my new church family one Sunday, and the Holy Spirit was moving. I was called to the front of the church, and they prayed for me. Before I knew it, I felt a touch on my forehead. I was lying on the floor. While lying on the floor, I heard as clear as day, "This is your home." I was not ready to accept that, so I continued to block it out. How could Pennsylvania be my home? I had a newly renovated apartment waiting for me in New York.

That evening, my children and I went back to New York to start our week all over again. I went to work at the nonprofit organization and spoke with the president. I wanted to know how long I would have to wait for the apartment to finish. He advised "Shortly."

I then went to my second job and was advised that they completed the contract and that would be my last day. But I was still okay financially. I was only down by one job.

Friday came, and I heard some amazing news. The apartment was finally completed. I rushed over to the property manager to see how soon I would be able to move into the apartment. When I arrived at her office, she gave such a sad look. I was confused because I thought the news to be great. It was great, but not for me. She then dropped the bomb on me. "Tammy, it is ready, but he told me not to give it to you. I'm sorry." I stood in awe. For almost a year, I waited for this apartment. The president of the company told me himself that it was mine. Yet now I was being told that he changed his mind.

I was so hurt. I finally had gotten to a place of truth. I finally said, "*No!*" to all things that was unpleasing to God. Why am I going through this God? After leaving her office, I came home. I went into the bathroom and closed the door. I looked into the mirror and began to speak to God.

"God, I don't understand. I know I am not perfect, but I have been trying my best to live right. It would be different if it was just me or me and one child. But God, it's me and my three babies. Every time I take a step forward, I find myself being pushed two steps back. I'm trying God and I can't seem to get ahead. I'm drowning here God. I know what you promised me, and I still believe you. This just hurts so bad. I don't know what I am doing. I don't even have the words right now. All I can say is, this hurts."

As the tears ran down my face, I began to remember Pennsylvania and what I learned in church and from the two powerhouse women. My prayer changed to, "Well, God, I trust and lean on you. You said you would never leave me or forsake me. You said that you have given me power. You said I can speak to the mountain, which will be removed. You said anything I ask in your name, I shall have it. So, Lord, I don't know how you are going to move or even when, but before this night ends, I need you to show up and show out. I need to see your hand move before the day is over." I wiped my tears and got myself ready to go to church and teach the choir.

When the rehearsal was over, I heard a still small voice say, "Go by Pathmark." This was a supermarket. Now, let me stop here. We must be mindful of "Prepositions." These words may have few letters, but they are very powerful, especially pertaining to instructions.

At first, I did not catch it. I thought I could stand to go to Pathmark and pick up some groceries. I started walking towards Pathmark and just before I could enter, a woman came out with her husband and their children. They were carrying grocery bags. The woman said hi, and I also responded with a hi. She then asked if I would allow her to speak with me. I said "ok."

She seemed to be ever so gentle until she said "You are so hardheaded! Why do you think that everything is drying up for you here? It's because it's time for you to go! Do you know where you are supposed to go?" I answered in a small voice, "yes." She then said, "Then goodbye!"

That night, I knew where I was going. She did what God had instructed her to do, and she did not leave any space for questions or even a hug. She walked away with her family.

Chapter 27

Time To Transition

It excited me that God provided me with a clear answer. I was no longer confused, but I was nervous. How was this going to work out? I would need to get a job in Pennsylvania, have the first month's rent with a security deposit. The biggest issue was that Mister had a court order visitation to have the children every other weekend. Despite the many thoughts that ran through my mind, I was glad for direction.

I held what God had revealed to me until Sunday morning. I called my godmother on my way to direct a choir in the Bronx. When she answered the phone I said, "Good morning god mommy."

And before I could say anything else, she responded, "The Lord told me that you were on your way! See you tomorrow!" She then hung up.

I found myself standing completely still in the middle of the sidewalk. I was in shock and at the same time overwhelmed with joy. God was showing me that I was special to him and even though I may not have known all that he was doing, he was definitely working it all out for my good. I was so grateful.

Because it was now summer, my children were out of school. We took a van service over to Allentown, Pennsylvania, and met up with my godmother and god sister. They soon confirmed that my children and I would move into my first apartment in August 2009.

There were many times I struggled to get to Pennsylvania from New York, but God always worked it out for me. My god brother and god sister sometimes drove to New York just to pick us up. It didn't matter about the time, but they remained faithful.

My brother and producer, "Big Moe," often made sure we made it to PA safely.

There was a wonderful woman by the name of Desiree, and she resided in Pennsylvania. She worked in New Jersey. On Fridays, my children and I would take the NJ Transit from New York Penn Station to Newark Penn Station and meet with her. She then drove us to Pennsylvania. She is no longer here with us but left an amazing legacy behind.

Many people stepped in to ensure I and my children were okay. I salute you all. I am forever grateful, and you will never be forgotten.

Sometimes I couldn't pay my rent and my god sister and godbrother carried me. The love they exemplified and still today is unmatched.

Through it all I was still going to court with Mister and one day he advised the judge that I moved to PA. She looked at me and said "Who do you think you are? Do you think that you are above the law? You cannot just go up and move with these kids to another state! Their father has rights." The more she spoke, the more I cried, and my heart dropped. She then said, "Are you listening to me?"

I answered, "Yes, your Honor."

She said, "Let me repeat myself because I want to make sure you are hearing me clearly."

I questioned God, "Was everything that I have done thus far for nothing? Why would you allow me to come this far to take it all away? What have I done to be punished like this?"

The judge then said, "You cannot just go up and move with these kids to another state! Their father has rights. You will need to file a petition for relocation. If you want to file a petition for relocation, you have to go across the hall. You cannot just do what you want to do!

Because you would need to GO ACROSS THE HALL TO ROOM 304!! You are not above the law! If you want to relocate to Pennsylvania, you need to file for it. You cannot just take matters into your own hands! Do you hear me?"

I soon realized what the judge was doing. "Yes, your Honor." (*smile*)

The sound of her delivery was quite harsh, but that was not important. Her words were. She provided me with instructions and at the same time she reminded me that I was not above the law.

I was tickled because Mister looked confused. I believe that he somewhat grasped what was happening, but still had doubts. My attorneys just sat in amazement with a smile.

The judge capped off the instructions by saying, "And make sure it's filed by the next appearance!"

After they dismissed us from the courtroom, I walked right on over to room 304 and filed the petition for relocation.

I did not stop traveling to PA. I was more encouraged that God was working in my favor. Even though I no longer had a steady job, I trusted God. I became Liberty Worship Center's first choir directress, and that was an amazing experience. It was a circle within itself because I started as a student, if you will, with my godmother at an early age, and now I as an adult came back to doing what I had been taught for so many years.

I continued to sing and teach music. Soon afterward, I started producing my plays again and ministering on the pulpit every now and again.

I found myself becoming stronger as a woman, a mother, and as a servant of God. Despite the ups and downs, I really believed that God was going to see me through.

CIRCLES

In one of the court proceedings, Mister stated that he thought that I was abusing our children, so he reached out to the police and shared this concern. This same judge stated that she found it awkward that out of all the times we have had court appearances, he did not mention this. She advised the courtroom deputy to do some research pertaining to my history. However, the judge did not stop there. She stated that she did not just want to know about me but Mister as well.

Because of this concern, I received a call from ACS located in New York City. They arranged a date and time to have someone meet me and my children at my apartment in Allentown, PA.

I remained prayerful! I was in a place of victory and not revenge. Even though I couldn't be considered officially a resident of PA because they did not grant me relocation, I would not stop trusting God. I have seen so many miracles and blessings. God freed me! I was not going to worry about what I saw with my natural eyes, but how great things were manifesting in the natural for me. God had a plan and even though I was not privy to the blueprints, I knew that he counted me as his own.

At my home in PA, I was in the process of cooking a roaster, macaroni & cheese, string beans, and cornbread. I left my slide door open to let out some of the heat from the kitchen. I heard a knock on the door. It was a woman from the ACS located in PA. I invited her in right after she asked, "Are you the one doing all that cooking? It smells amazing." (*smile*)

I showed her into my living room, and she was so impressed. See, I never understood this thing called credit, but apparently, 751 was a good score. That allowed me to purchase my living room, dining room, and bedroom sets.

She sat down on the sofa and interviewed my children, then she walked around the entire apartment with her clipboard. Finally, she stood inside my kitchen and asked me some questions. She soon placed her hand in the air and said, "Enough! I have seen and heard enough! If you ever need me, just call me!" and she left.

I did not know her thoughts, but I trusted the process. I soon began to hear that small, still voice again, and it said, "Now, you will need to keep your mouth shut. Do not talk about what you are going through. Do not talk about how you feel. Do not share any information about your views regarding Mister. Just live and keep moving! I am going to show you something."

I understood the instructions but did not understand the "why." I knew that it was God speaking and I was not going to disobey him.

When I returned to New York, I was riding the city bus and received a phone call. It was Teresa. She mentioned that we haven't talked in a while and asked how the children and I were doing. I answered that we were doing well. She then proceeded to say that we should go for coffee one day and talk. I agreed to the coffee but expressed that I was limited in what I would talk about. I expressed that we could definitely have some sister time, but I would not be discussing anything pertaining to the court, Mister, or what I was dealing with.

She expressed that she was bothered and thought of us to be sisters. I agreed, but I further expressed that these were instructions straight from God. We never had a cup of coffee.

On December 13, 2009, I attended Liberty Worship Center in PA. All my church family came together this Sunday and prayed for me and my children. We cried out to God together to move on me and my children's behalf. That service will always be remembered and shall go down in history. I remained with a pure heart. God had allowed me to not have a heart of hatred and to not hold anything in my heart against Mister. Outside of Mister, I was embarking on my journey, and God was merciful. God continued to bless me, but I understood that it was my duty to remain in the right posture with God.

That evening, my children and I rode back to New York so that they could attend school and I would be going to court on that Monday. December 14, 2009, came, and I made a phone call to my godmother. She prayed over me and through me. The power of the Holy Ghost fell on me, and I began speaking in tongues. I felt so much strength and power it was like I had become untouchable. I heard the Lord say, "Tammy, this will be your last day and I will show everyone who I am on this day and who you serve. Walk in your victory because YOU HAVE WON!"

I went to the courthouse a bit earlier that day to meet with my attorneys. When I arrived, I saw Mister, together with his parents, his brother, his attorney, the children's attorney, and Teresa. I was so overjoyed and on fire for God. I had so much love in my heart that day because I knew I had won. It did not matter how many people were against me, but they couldn't compare to the God that was for me.

Teresa walked over to me to explain that she was there because the children's attorney asked her to be there. It did not matter! I was good.

God said he was going to show himself that day. I felt like I was walking as a little girl holding onto my daddy's hand and I was walking him into a space where the bullies were waiting to jump me. I would then tell my daddy, "Get them daddy! There they are! Those are the ones that messed with me!" and my daddy would sho nuff take care of them for messing with his baby.

We went over what they expected after I approached my attorneys. I then advised them both that it wasn't going to happen that way today. I explained that I understood that they had been in this field for 25-plus years, but this was going to be the last time that I would need to attend court.

One of the attorneys looked at me sadly and said, "I'm so sorry. It doesn't work that way. Relocation is a hard type of case to win, and it takes several court appearances to get it approved. I commend you on your courage and belief, but it's not a reality." I then responded, "When I win today, I want you to come back to me and say, who is this God you serve?"

The judge then called all the attorneys in and, after about ten minutes, they all returned and went to their respective places. My attorneys looked a bit confused. One then stated, "If we granted you relocation, you would be responsible for the children traveling back and forth to New York. Are you willing to take on that responsibility?"

My answer was "Yes!"

They then went back into the courtroom, and the doors were closed. Another five minutes had passed and then the judge requested us to come in as well.

Suddenly, Mister and everyone with him started to enter the courtroom. The judge stopped everyone and said she only wanted to see Mister and me. We entered the courtroom and the judge then said, "So, you want to relocate to Pennsylvania, right?"

I answered, "Yes, your honor."

The judge then said, "I am going to give you an early Christmas present. I am granting you and your children relocation to Pennsylvania!" It did not surprise me that God was going to show out. I looked at my attorneys and they were speechless. They just kept looking at each other in disbelief.

On the other hand, Mister was very upset and kept saying, "What?!"

I walked out of the courtroom and met with my attorneys. One of the attorneys stated that she has never witnessed anything like this in her life and walked away. The second attorney just stared at me. I then reminded her of the question I was waiting to hear. "Who is this God you serve?" She couldn't find a way to say those words, but from her response, I knew that experience changed her life."

I walked by myself to the elevator. I was not scared! I WAS VICTORIOUS! If God allowed me to be untouchable in the courthouse, I was going to remain untouchable outside the courthouse. I was no longer living my life in fear but in truth and boldness.

I went to my mother's house and shared that I had won. My mother was angry, hurt, and relieved all at once. Hurt because I never shared my journey and maybe she could have protected me a bit more. Angry because had she known she wouldn't have been so nice to Mister. Relieved because I survived! I finally sat down and shared my story that I ran from for so many years.

I allowed my children to finish school for the year, and we left New York once the Christmas break came.

Chapter 28

Break The Chains

Moving to PA was a breath of fresh air for me. I learned how to stand on my own two feet there. I learned to face my fears head-on. The first true church family that I found was there. It was where I found my now husband. It was where I found my voice. I still made mistakes and had some ups and downs in PA, but it all contributed to my journey. It still took time for me to love myself and to know myself. It took time for me to know what I wanted out of this thing called life. People had spoken so many bad things over me, I struggled not to believe them.

I sometimes struggled as a mother because I couldn't give my children things, I didn't have myself. I couldn't teach them they were special because I did not believe I was. I couldn't teach them that they were more than enough because I felt less than. I couldn't speak life over them because I was being drained. I started to believe that I had to become tougher on them because I wanted them to be better and do better than me. However, they did not need my toughness or coldness. They needed to be held and loved. They needed what seemed to be so simple, but it was the absolute hardest for me because I did not know what love was to give love.

I grew up understanding that if I was fed, had clothes on my back, and a roof over my head that was love. But in writing this book, I understood that some parents do the best they can with what they have, and we cannot fault them for that. When you know better, you do better. YOU BREAK THE CHAINS!

I pray that you have seen purpose in my writing. Things in life have left us broken, bruised, and battered. Life at times seemed to be so hard, it was easier to just give up and die. We have made many mistakes and feel as if there is no way to recover. Who likes starting over? I didn't!

But I beseech thee, my sister. No matter what you have suffered through or maybe suffering through right now, there is a purpose for your life and your journey. I need you to know that you are somebody special and you do not have to settle. THERE IS MORE! No matter what has been spoken over you. No matter how hard it may be for you to see it. YOU ARE! DO NOT GIVE UP! NO MATTER HOW MANY TIMES YOU FALL (and you will) CRAWL until you can WALK until you can RUN until you can FLY until you can SOAR!

Abuse comes in many shapes and sizes. You may not know all the signs or even if it's considered abuse. But if anything, or anyone makes you uncomfortable, do not keep it to yourself. The abuser has power only if you give it to them. Take a stand, be a voice, and know that you are fearfully and wonderfully made. (Psalm 139:14)

I now reside in Virginia and have remarried. I now own two businesses, Jus Tammy, LLC, and Bridging the Gaps For Queens, Inc. As of 2019, I became a gospel recording artist. For the first time in my life attending college at the age of 46, I graduated with Highest Honors (Magna Cum Laude) from Tidewater Community College on May 8, 2023, with my degree in Small Business Management and Entrepreneurship.

All three of my biological children are doing well. My daughter graduated from high school and is blessing me with my second grandbaby. She has a heart of gold. My mom is her best friend. She is also my make-up, fashion, and hair artist. Not to mention her voice is definitely something worth listening to. My oldest son graduated from high school with honors and is now attending college alongside me as he works to establish himself as independent. My youngest son will graduate high school with honors in June 2023. His GPA is almost 4.0, and he hasn't determined if he will attend college immediately, but he has already created three businesses.

My husband has blessed me with five more children and eight grandchildren. God has blessed me with a bigger family, and I love every one of them to my core.

My children and I attended many therapy sessions, individually and as a family. Yes, I trust God and every word he has spoken, but it was and still is important to understand that sometimes we need a human being to help us figure out some things. God doesn't come down and speak to us directly. Instead, he works through people. This is why Christ gave some apostles, prophets, evangelists, pastors, and teachers. (Eph 4:11)

To succeed in life, I had to accept the fact that I needed help. My children needed to understand that being hurt, angry, and confused was okay. I couldn't fix them because I was still broken.

Because of therapy and my gradual spiritual maturity in God, I am now able to tell my children that I love them without feeling like it is a sign of weakness. I have been able to be open and honest about my feelings, colorful past, and mistakes. I have granted them the safe space to speak their peace with me as well. It is no longer do as I say but do as I do and better.

There is power in taking accountability. With this power, nothing or no one can come along and make you believe differently. For them to become great in life, I had to take accountability for my screw-ups, which in turn helped them to take accountability for what they could do better in their life. Regarding Mister, he and I are able to be cordial. We have been able to celebrate our children together and respect that even though we did not work out, God still has a purpose for our lives.

In February 2023, my mom turned 70 years old. She has been the strongest and most powerful influence in my life. She has taught me perseverance and survival. I love and appreciate every lesson she has taught me.

Even though I was molested in my younger years, I have forgiven them. Sometimes we look at the act, but have you ever considered the "why?" Sometimes people do things because it was done to them as well. This is not to make an excuse but to open your way of thinking.

As of to date, my father is still alive. He remarried and stopped drinking for three years. I learned they officially diagnosed him with schizophrenia and bipolar. He did well for approximately three years and then he relapsed. As of to date, he is back in prison, and I don't know for how long this time, but I can say that those three years we've had were the absolute best years of my life in having a father. I cried to him. I trusted him and took advice from him. He ministered to me at times and prayed over me. I truly miss him, BUT God is giving me strength.

All my siblings are doing amazing things and have blessed me with the best nieces and nephews I could have ever had.

I never received an apology from anyone concerning any negative roles they may have played in my life. But I forgive them all without any regrets. Why? Because our God has forgiven us for ALL our sins (Hebrews 1:3). We do not have the right to not forgive someone no matter how terrible things may have been. Count it all joy (James 1:2) for all things work together for good to them that love God, to them who are called according to his purpose (Romans 8:2) When you forgive, you are now free. YOU HAVE THE POWER TO BREAK THE CHAINS!

Dear God,

I am grateful for this opportunity that you have given me to bring hope to the hopeless, to shed light in the darkness, and to acknowledge your power boldly. I pray that you reveal yourself to everyone reading this book and that every chain is broken and released from their lives, never to return. In Jesus' name, Amen!

Self-Reflective Questions:

1. What are the chains in my life I need to be freed from?

_____

_____

_____

_____

2. Am I holding on to something I need to let go of?

_____

_____

_____

_____

3. Am I living true to myself?

_____

_____

_____

_____

4. Am I sacrificing my happiness to make someone else happy?

_____

_____

_____

_____

4. Am I allowing myself to settle?

_____

_____

_____

_____

5. Am I achieving the goals that I have set for myself?

_____

_____

_____

_____

6. If I could encourage my younger self, what would I say?

_____

_____

_____

_____

7. If this were the last day of my life, would I have the same plans for today?

_____

_____

_____

_____

8. When was the last time I challenged myself to step out of my comfort zone?

_____

_____

_____

_____

9. What do I need to change about myself?

_____

_____

_____

_____

10. Is it more important to love or to be loved?

_____

_____

_____

_____

11. Which is worse: failing or never trying?

_____

_____

_____

_____

12. Who am I, really?

_____

_____

_____

_____

13. Am I willing to start all over?

_____

_____

_____

_____

14. What matters the most to me in my life?

_____

_____

_____

_____

Daily Affirmations:

- I am free
- I am a survivor
- I am me, unapologetically.
- I am who God says I am
- I am fearfully and wonderfully made
- I am victorious and more than a conqueror
- I am stronger than I think.
- I am releasing guilt
- I am breaking generational cycles
- I am not defined by my past but driven by my future
- I am getting better and better each day
- I am focused
- I am enough
- I am worthy of investing in myself
- I am unstoppable
- I am rising above thoughts that are trying to make me angry or afraid
- I am turning down the volume of negativity in my life, while simultaneously turning up the volume of positivity
- I am in charge of my own identity and destiny
- I am allowed to change my mind
- I am proud of myself

Self-Love:

I LOVE MYSELF JUST AS I AM TODAY

I CHOOSE TO BE KIND TO MYSELF

I APPRECIATE ALL THE WAYS THAT I AM UNIQUE

ALL I NEED IS WITHIN ME RIGHT NOW

I CAN BE WHATEVER I WANT TO BE

I USE OBSTACLES TO MOTIVATE ME TO LEARN AND GROW

I FORGIVE MYSELF AND FREE MYSELF

I DESERVE TO FORGIVE AND BE FORGIVEN

I WILL STOP APOLOGIZING FOR THINGS I CAN'T CONTROL

MY LEADERSHIP MAKES A DIFFERENCE

I DO NOT HAVE TO BE HAPPY ALL THE TIME

IT'S OKAY NOT TO HAVE IT ALL TOGETHER

IT'S OKAY TO START ALL OVER

Declarations:

TODAY IS A PHENOMENAL DAY

TODAY WILL BE A PRODUCTIVE DAY

EACH AND EVERY DAY, I AM GETTING CLOSER TO ACHIEVING MY GOALS

I'VE MADE IT THROUGH HARD TIMES BEFORE, AND I'VE COME OUT STRONGER AND BETTER BECAUSE OF THEM.

I WILL MAKE IT THROUGH THIS.

THERE IS AN INCREDIBLE POWER I POSSESS WITHIN ME TO ACHIEVE ANYTHING I DESIRE

NOTE TO SELF: I AM GOING TO MAKE YOU SO PROUD

I FEED MY SPIRIT. I TRAIN MY BODY. I FOCUS MY MIND. THIS IS MY TIME.

ONE SMALL POSITIVE THOUGHT IN THE MORNING CAN CHANGE MY WHOLE DAY.

TODAY I RISE WITH A POWERFUL THOUGHT TO SET THE TONE AND ALLOW SUCCESS TO REVERBERATE THROUGH EVERY MOMENT OF MY DAY.

I STAND UP FOR MYSELF

I CAN DO HARD THINGS

MY IDEAS ARE POWERFUL

TODAY I WILL TAKE MY FIRST STEP

I WILL SURPASS ALL EXPECTATIONS

I HAVE A VOICE

I WILL NOT SETTLE

About The Author

Tammy Flowers-Hollis, also known as Jus Tammy, was born in Camden, SC, and raised in the vibrant city of New York. Being the second of five children, Tammy's incredible talent was evident from a young age. She became known for her petite stature and powerful voice at just four years old. By age 11, Tammy had already recorded her first album with an all-woman gospel group called, "The Voices of New York." Her musical journey continued as she performed off-Broadway and in various musical productions, solidifying her love for the arts.

Fueling her creativity and expanding her repertoire, Tammy delved into writing and producing plays. Alongside her theatrical pursuits, she continued to share her soul-stirring vocals on various radio programs while dedicating over 15 years as a cherished choir director. Tammy's passion and dedication to her craft led her to record her second album, collaborating with "The Anointed Voices" under the guidance of Maurice (Big Moe) Bowles.

However, Tammy's life took a dramatic turn when she bravely left an abusive marriage after enduring a decade of turmoil. This pivotal moment ignited her calling to shed light on the grim reality of domestic violence. As a staunch advocate for domestic violence awareness, Tammy founded the nonprofit organization **Bridging the Gaps For Queens**. This impactful 501(c)(3) organization offers vital resources and support to women who have experienced domestic violence and sexual assault, equipping them with the tools to reintegrate as productive members of society.

In the summer of 2023, Tammy will release her highly anticipated book, *Circles: Breaking The Chains of Generational Curses*. This motivational memoir will captivate readers as they embark on a transformative journey through Tammy's life, learning valuable lessons along the way. Through her words, readers will be inspired to read, listen, learn, and grow.

Tammy's extraordinary talent has led her to share the stage with renowned gospel figures such as Hezekiah Walker, Bobby Jones, and John P. Kee. She has also graced the company of esteemed artists like Marvin Sapp, Jermaine Dolly, Isabel Davis, Nah-Tarsha Cherry, and many others. Tammy's musical accomplishments include the release of her first single, *Victorious*, under Cisum Music Productions on June 5, 2018. As of March 5, 2021, she assumed the role of CEO and Founder of Jus Tammy, LLC, and shortly after, on March 19, 2021, dropped her second scorching single, *Face2Face*. Brace yourselves, for Tammy has yet another sensational single set to release in the summer of 2023, promising to elevate listeners to unprecedented heights.

Walking the streets unapologetically, Tammy embraces her true self and the battle scars she carries. Authentic and genuine, she is simply Tammy—*JusTammy*—delivering her message with unwavering authenticity.

To contact the author:

 Facebook: JusTammyOfficial

 Instagram: JusTammyMusic

Email: OfficialJusTammy@gmail.com
Website: www.JusTammy.com

www.ingramcontent.com/pod-product-compliance
Lightning Source LLC
Chambersburg PA
CBHW071152120626
46546CB00006B/2232